STOWE

2

3

Stowe

Classic New England

By Peter Oliver

MOUNTAIN SPORTS PRESS

STOWE: Classic New England

Published by
Mountain Sports Press

Distributed to the book trade by:
PUBLISHERS GROUP WEST

Bill Grout, *Editor-in-Chief*
Michelle Klammer Schrantz, *Art Director*
Annie W. Krause, *Photo Editor*
Chris Salt, *Production Manager*
Alan Stark, *Associate Publisher*
Scott Kronberg, *Associate Art Director*
Andy Hawk, *Sales Representative*

Stowe Mountain Resort®
is a registered trademark of Mt. Mansfield Company, Inc.

ISBN 0-9717748-1-1
Library of Congress Cataloging-in-Publication Data applied for.

Printed in Canada
By Friesens Corporation

A subsidiary of:
TIME4MEDIA

929 Pearl Street, Suite 200
Boulder, CO 80302
303-448-7617

This book is dedicated to the memory

of Stowe skiing's visionaries—

Charlie Lord,

Roland Palmedo,

Sepp Ruschp

and C.V. Starr.

Their likes in skiing may never be seen again.

CONTENTS

FOREWORD

It's no use trying to reach me by phone on a winter morning. Look for me instead on Mt. Mansfield, Stowe's main mountain.

I have skied many of the world's great resorts, but Stowe always draws me home. Even when I have plans to sleep in, or to work, an internal predawn alarm clock rousts me out of bed. By first light I'm in my truck, and out of my Stowe Hollow driveway, eight miles from the skiing.

I pass the elementary school, the library, the white columns and steeple of the Stowe Community Church, the centerpiece of the waking village. At the Green Mountain Inn, which predates the Stowe Mountain Resort itself, I turn right onto the Mountain Road, lined with lodges, inns, shops, restaurants and pubs. I pass the road to the Trapp Family Lodge, where those *Sound of Music* refugees from Nazi occupation in Austria eventually settled—and went on to set high standards for hospitality.

Early as I might be at the Mt. Mansfield base, I'm never the first to arrive. I refuse to "do boots" in the parking lot, preferring to sit next to the fireplace in The Den, the oldest wing of the base lodge built by the Civilian Conservation Corps (who also cut the original runs) in the 1930s. But I might not find a seat.

Summer tourism in Stowe is now bigger than winter tourism. But the mountain remains the town's cultural focal point. Mt. Mansfield is the magnet that attracted so many locals, and then held them here. Stowe's population is top heavy with ski and snowboard aficionados (including Jake Burton Carpenter, the founder and CEO of Burton), racers and ski instructors past and present. Many come out early in the day, before drifting off to real jobs. For some, the goal is to make 10 runs on the high-speed lift by 10:00 a.m.

Light and snow are best in the morning. On powder days, several dozen, maybe hundreds, will be lined up at the main lifts by 7:30 looking to make first tracks. If nearby Lake Champlain is still free of ice, Mansfield may receive a fresh skim of snow from a lake-effect squall—a small bonus no other mountain in the area will enjoy. At the very least, I expect a near-perfect corduroy surface, after snowmakers and groomers have applied their overnight wizardry.

It's often said, "If you can ski Stowe, you can ski anywhere." Mt. Mansfield is most famous for its steep, narrow runs known as the Front Four. I confess that, on all but the most forgiving days, I shy from the cliff-like pitches of Starr, National and Goat, though I will ski the fourth challenge, Lift Line, most mornings.

I might warm up on Lord, the run named after Charlie Lord, who used his unerring sense of terrain, fall line, sun angle and wind direction to cut the original trails on Mt.

by Stu Campbell
SKI Magazine

Mansfield. Charlie's lyrical runs, tucked into the softer folds, humps and rocky skeleton of the mountain, were so flawless they have changed little in 65 years. They seem to embrace me as I ski them.

I often ski by myself in the early light. But I'm not alone. The morning pace is fast, and the mountain, as it always has, crawls with skiing role models. There are racers from the Mt. Mansfield Ski Club, University of Vermont and nearby ski academies (some of them destined to be Olympians), instructors making warm-up laps, testers and technicians from ski and snowboard companies like Burton, Dynastar, Rossignol, Elan and Völkl.

I sense the lingering presence of champions like Toni Sailer and Jean-Claude Killy, who raced and won here. I see the ghosts of celebrities and figures like the Kennedys, who were frequent guests here. I'm joined by the spirit of Sepp Ruschp, imported from Austria to be Stowe's first ski school director, and by his successor, Kerr Sparks, who was both mentor and father figure to me.

In the early days of the Stowe Mountain Resort, known then as the Mt. Mansfield Company, Ruschp and Sparks went to the remote valleys of Austria to seek the handsomest, most competent ski instructors they could find. The instructors came, dined with guests in the Lodge at Smuggler's Notch and Toll House Inn, worked their magic with struggling stem-turners, and established a tradition of instructional excellence at Stowe that persists into the 21st century.

Some mornings in Stowe can be cold and windy. Yet I almost never look out the window and assume the skiing is bad. I go to the mountain anyway, and nestle comfortably into the ambiance and camaraderie there. As many Stoweites will tell you, the skiing's often best on the most unlikely of days.

My morning on the mountain will end after the fresh snow is tracked out or the smooth corduroy is consumed. As ski school classes form at the bases of Mt. Mansfield and Spruce Peak, as eager guests and their families start to swell the lift lines, I think about taking off my boots and going back to my home office in Stowe Hollow.

Sometimes I don't. During the busiest weeks, I hang around. Pressed into service like many semi-retired instructors who live here, I slip into a red uniform and resume the role of ski teacher, one I cherished (seven days a week) years ago. I can't do it full time now, but I still think I'd rather teach than eat.

Yes, most winter days you can reach me at home. Just not before lunch.

STOWE HOLLOW, APRIL, 2002

STOWE *Introduction*

What a day it was: The morning dawning clear and abnormally warm, full of promise. March in northern Vermont is a month that regularly gets its seasonal signals crossed, as snowy winter collides with the balmy coming of spring. More often than not, winter gets the best of that collision. But on this day, in March 1967, as I prepared to encounter Stowe skiing for the first time in my life, spring had moved in with total command.

The temperature rose with the sun, breaching the 40-degree mark by eight in the morning and not stopping in its steady climb toward 60 degrees. The lowland cornfields were flooded with snowmelt, and the air at around 4,000 feet—the approximate summit elevation of Stowe's

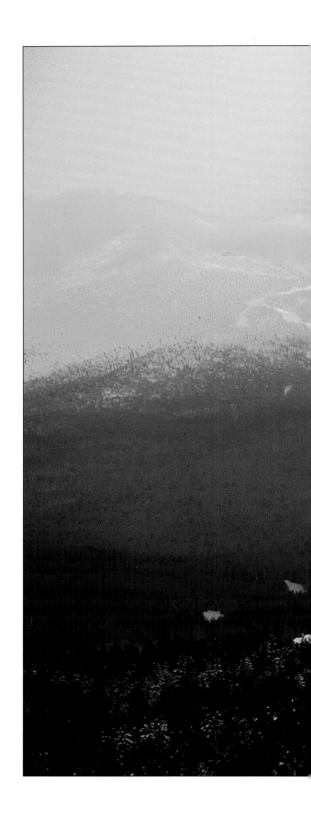

Mt. Mansfield—was consumed in the kind of diaphanous, pale blue haze that comes when the cold temperatures of dwindling mountain snow meet the high-angled, vernal sun.

My cousin, my brothers and I had driven up to Stowe that morning from my family's house, about an hour to the south. My cousin, having only recently acquired his driver's license, was confident if not entirely steady behind the wheel. As we neared Stowe on Route 100, Mt. Mansfield began to grow as a commanding presence on the northwestern horizon, its treeless summit crowned with a pale sheen of white snow and ice. It was like no other mountain I'd ever seen in the East—a reasonable facsimile, I imagined, of something I might encounter in the Rockies. It was taller, whiter, more imposing and thoroughly more impressive than the other Green Mountains I was familiar with. Just driving up the Mountain Road and seeing that brute of a mountain in front of us, we figured we'd entered the big leagues of Eastern skiing.

Spring fever was rampantly contagious that day. As the temperature soared, clothing was shed to—and sometimes beyond—the point of minimalism. Flower-print windshirts, representing the height of skiing fashion at the time, were the attire of choice for those who chose to remain clothed. From the deck of the Octagon, the lodge below the mountaintop protuberance known as the Nose, people with wineskins were squirting long streams of liquid refreshment in the approximate direction of open mouths passing nearby on the parallel single and double chairlifts.

The moguls on National, the most heavily moguled of Stowe's famous Front Four trails, were as soft and malleable as any moguls I'd ever encountered before. Elsewhere, the soft snow allowed a headstrong adolescent like me to blast with confidence down steeps that in midwinter—under drier, colder and icier conditions—would demand no-nonsense caution.

In flatter places toward the bottom of the mountain, pools of slush formed, and some people were building jumps in order to leap right into the frigid glop. Being young and not entirely sensible, I, too, took the plunge, which turned out not to be such a crazy idea after all. The initial shock of the cold water was swept away by solar warmth intense enough to dry you out within minutes—all in all, something like a sauna in reverse. The whole day turned into an outrageous, free-spirited, sometimes lunatic romp, still one of the greatest days of skiing I've ever experienced.

The Ski Capital of the East—that's the title Stowe conferred upon itself in those days, a title it still claims. The title was obviously conjured up as a public-relations device, an attempt to establish some sort of claim to being better than all the other guys.

I'll allow the Stowe folks a little breast-beating, because the claim wasn't without merit. Here, in Mt. Mansfield, was Vermont's tallest mountain, at 4,395 feet. Here was where big-mountain skiing in Vermont was really born, in the mid '30s. Here in a cluster of trails known as the Front Four—National, Goat, Starr and Lift Line—was probably the preeminent challenge in Eastern skiing.

Here was the essential New England ski town, with its church steeple and clapboard houses and an aura of skiing tradition wafting around every street corner. Here, in some of its most famous migrants (e.g., the von Trapp family and Sepp Ruschp) was a direct link to the world of the Alps and all the weighty import that that brought to skiing. Stowe had the goods. It still does.

When I first visited Stowe in 1967, the ski area had the deserved reputation of being essentially an experts-only place, despite the presence of smaller, gentler Spruce Peak alongside Mt. Mansfield. The experts-only feeling would impress itself upon you even before you ever put skis to snow. The big S in the ubiquitous Stowe logo was drawn with a swashbuckling swoosh full of boldness and gumption, and just the name itself—Stowe—had a single-syllable, uncompromising toughness to it. It had the sound of a blunt, well-delivered body blow for anyone who wasn't up to the high standard the mountain demanded.

In the decades since the '60s, of course, Stowe has undergone considerable change. Just a year after my 1967 visit, the first gondola was built. It was a watershed moment in the area's expansion, opening up a whole new swath of intermediate terrain and making Mt. Mansfield's appeal more broad based.

The arrival of the gondola and the intermediate terrain it served didn't defang Mt. Mansfield's experts-only image; the Front Four were still the Front Four. But the image and reality of Stowe were unquestionably softened. Now Mom and the kids no longer had to be shuttled off to Spruce Peak while the men of the family did battle on Mt. Mansfield. The whole family could now ski the big mountain.

This conversion, from expert's to everyman's ski area, was part of Stowe's steady flow into the mainstream of skiing tourism. The conversion was emblematic of an important transformation that took place not just in Stowe but in Vermont in general in the latter third of the 20th century. Tourism, driven in no small part by skiing, began to take over as king of the state economy. Such industries as farming, marble mining, logging and maple sugaring receded in importance as tourism established itself as Vermont's number-one money-maker.

Stowe was no latecomer to this trend; in fact, for many years it was well ahead of the curve in courting tourism. Summer tourists were coming in considerable numbers by the second half of the 1800s, drawn by (among other attractions) Mt. Mansfield's Summit House, built in 1858, and the Toll Road up to the summit

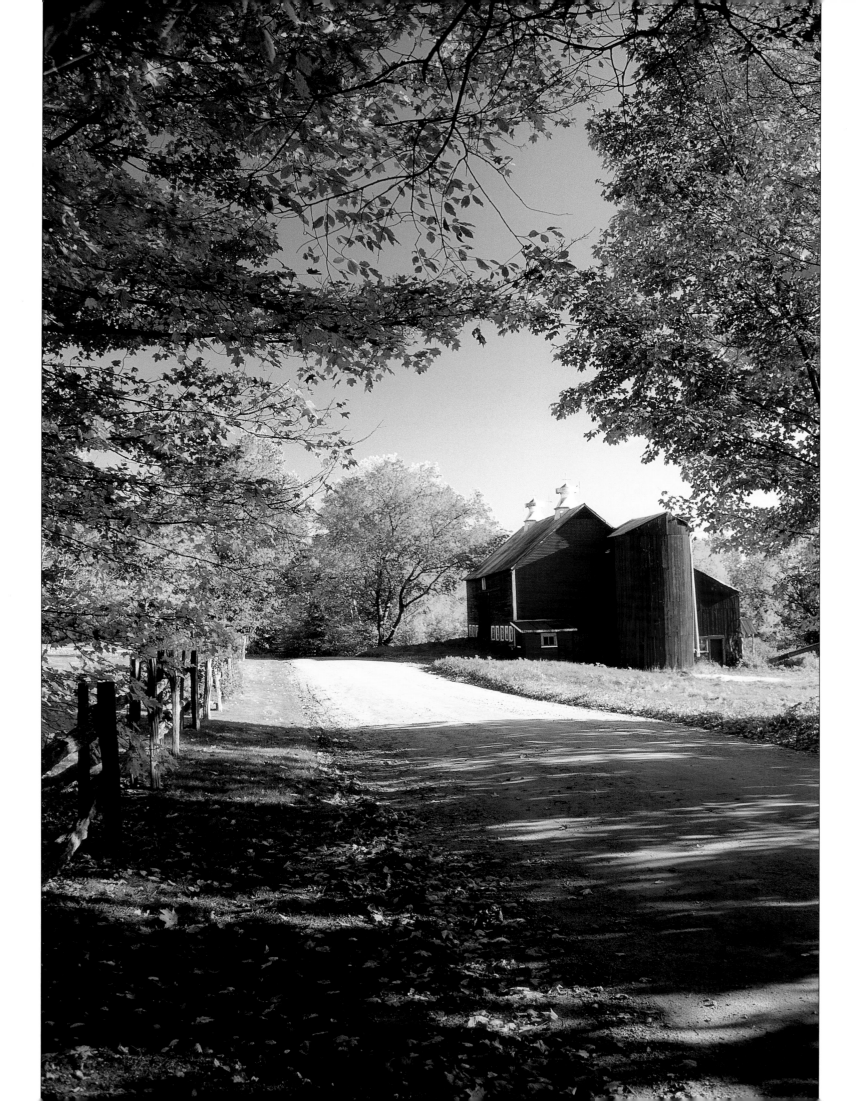

ridge. In the pre-automotive era, horse-drawn carriages were the main means of transport in bringing visitors to the grand views and fresh air afforded by Mansfield's summit.

Winter tourism would follow some years later. The first Stowe Winter Carnival was held in 1921, at least a decade before downhill skiing in the United States, or anywhere else, would become popular. On the road to tourism, Stowe has been the pacesetter among Vermont communities.

These days, Stowe—and here I bundle together the mountain, the village and the surrounding area under the single name—is a larger, more sprawling, more commercial place than it was when I first arrived in the mid '60s. Along the Mountain Road, which leads from the village of Stowe to the ski area, there are many more stores, restaurants and inns.

For the most part, the Mountain Road development is a tasteful array of clapboard siding, occasional ersatz-Tyrolean structures reflecting the area's Alpine connections and signs made of painted wood. (Give Vermont credit for its state law banning ostentatious billboards.) The products for sale might be T-shirts, trinkets, cheesy landscape paintings and scented candles, just as you might find in any tourist hub. But at least they're sold in establishments that retain considerable respect for the architectural traditions of New England. Stowe's 21st-century wares seem to fold in comfortably with the elements of Stowe that date back three centuries.

Of course it can seem at times a bit studied and contrived— dolling up an image of bucolic Vermont as part of a carefully crafted campaign to attract more visitors. But perhaps I'm overly cynical in saying so. Even as Stowe aggressively courts the holy tourism dollar, it has managed to retain the look and spirit of an attractively down-to-earth place.

Furthermore, as you exit Stowe to the north on Route 100, headed toward Morrisville, rural Vermont reasserts itself. The land flattens and the valley fans out. Cornfields, silos and cows deep in muck quickly become the constituent elements of the landscape. The accompanying aromas are there too, just for olfactory confirmation. Before dawn every morning—even before ski conditions are reported—the local radio station airs dairy reports, with updates on current wholesale milk prices, bovine metabolic disorders and other information that only a farmer could love. Agriculture may now play second fiddle to tourism in Vermont, but even in an area like Stowe, dominated by tourism, it can still claim its rightful place.

To see this relatively comfortable integration of skiing, tourism and rural life reinforces my appreciation for the unique character of New England skiing in general and Stowe skiing specifically. In the West and even in many parts of the Alps, most major ski resorts have been created as little more than that: resorts for skiing. They are like satellites come to rest on a foreign landscape, self-contained colonies dedicated to skiing but with otherwise little connection to the world around them.

Take Vail, Colorado, for example. The town of Vail was born entirely as a support system for the ski area, which came into being in 1962. The whole entity—comprising lodges, restaurants, hotels, lifts and so on—was, from its inception, a resort and nothing else. In France, similar resorts, such as Courchevel and Tignes, are said to be purpose-built, an unabashed admission that they were created for no purpose other than skiing. While Vail in its 40-year growth has gradually broadened its cultural horizons, skiing (and affiliated tourism) is still the core element of its social and economic existence.

I say this not necessarily as criticism but as a means of providing contrast. Rather than developing through modern resort planning, skiing in New England has evolved ad hoc. Long before the arrival of skiing, there were towns that had nothing to do with skiing—towns with their own preexisting character, traditions, social customs and economic raison d'être. Skiing first nudged its way into this rural ethos in the '30s and proceeded to grow over the years, through a kind of organic process, into becoming just one (albeit an important) part of the larger canvas of winter life.

A typical New England ski-area history might go like this: A bunch of gung ho guys would form a ski club. Many of these young pioneers would probably be graduates of small New England colleges like Dartmouth, Williams and Middlebury, where enthusiasm for the outdoors ran high. They would head to mountains and, without having to worry too much about stringent permitting laws back then, would cut a few trees down to create trails on which to ski. With the '30s being tough economic times, they'd probably get a helping hand in their trail cutting from a government-sponsored make-work group like the Civilian Conservation Corps.

Pretty soon, with interest in skiing growing, a demand to learn the new sport would lead to the development of a ski school. Administration of the school would often fall into the hands of someone of Alpine origin, where the beginnings of skiing pedagogy were fast developing. For an aspiring ski-school entrepreneur from, say, Austria, coming to the United States in the '30s was, not incidentally, a way of escaping the escalation of war in Europe.

Growing popularity would also spur a demand for more convenient uphill transport, because how many people were willing to hike back up after every run? So the young pioneers would cobble together some contraption built with an old automobile

engine and hardware-store rope. They would charge less than a dollar a day for the privilege of using the tow, and with that, the rudiments of a commercial ski industry—trails, lifts, ski school, lift tickets—were in place.

Over the years, more trails would be cut, lift technology would improve, and a club-style management would give way to something more commercial and professional. In the process, skiing would gradually weave itself into the social and cultural fabric of the area. But there was in the beginning no grand resort scheme, no master plan.

This, more or less, is the story of Stowe, the archetypal tale of New England skiing. Today, Stowe remains perhaps the classic New England paradigm of a ski area and village that have grown together, now coexisting symbiotically.

I happen to like that, even if it means sacrificing such resort-like conveniences as slopeside lodging, a big selling point for major Western resorts. The fact that skiing is an integral part of Stowe life rather than the single focus somehow invigorates the experience of spending time there.

To be sure, on your average winter weekend in Stowe, skiers are everywhere and skiing is the theme du jour. The bustle of tourism commerce is vigorous and unavoidable, and it's not always greeted with open arms. More than a few local residents complain, for example, about the influx of second-home wealth and out-of-staters coming in and wrecking the neighborhood. They claim, not without justification, that out-of-state wealth has pushed real-estate values beyond the level of affordability. Vermonters in general have cultivated an enduring tradition of

eyeing out-of-staters with suspicion, even though Vermonters born out of state now outnumber those born within.

Still, amid the tourist influx and the debate about the tourist influx, there beats in Stowe the persistent pulse of a rural Vermont community. That this is possible even in one of Vermont's prime tourism hubs speaks volumes about the importance that the state and its residents place on maintaining links to a deep-rooted rural heritage. Various state laws—the sometimes controversial Act 250 in particular—are Vermont's legislative way of welcoming change only at arm's length. Both culturally and politically, Vermont is disinclined to let go of its rural character easily.

The skiing, however, is the thing that keeps bringing me back to Stowe. Stowe has the whole package, as the saying goes. Hard skiing, easy skiing, the best cross-country network in Vermont—you name it, Stowe has it in abundance.

And, of course, an abundance of snow as well. The season begins early and lasts long. In a typical year, the first measurable snow falls on Mt. Mansfield in late September, with snow lasting on the mountaintop until June. The average annual snowfall exceeds 250 inches, and in the epic winter of 2000-01, 388 inches fell. By March of that winter, the natural-snow depth high on the mountain was more than 10 feet.

Stowe's challenging terrain and abundant snow have historically attracted a legion of great skiers. For many years, racing was at the heart of Stowe culture; running the downhill on the Nose Dive trail was considered one of the great tests in American skiing. The International, held for several years in the '50s, was an event that regularly brought to Stowe the very best racers in the world. Such stars as Billy Kidd, the first U.S. man to win an Olympic medal in Alpine skiing (in 1964), were raised on Stowe skiing.

Racing has receded somewhat from the forefront, at Stowe and elsewhere in America, but New England's best skiers continue to hold Stowe in the highest regard. That combination of terrain and snow remains hard to beat. And with advances in skier ability and equipment (toward shorter, wider boards with more sidecut) and the advent of snowboarding, the mountain seems to present a bigger, more complex web of challenges than ever. As skiers and riders seek an element of adventure they can't find on well-maintained trails, the woods between trails and other off-trail terrain are now clearly in the mix.

This growing exploratory zeal, entangled in environmental and safety concerns, has raised more than a few hackles. That should come as no surprise in a state like Vermont, where public land use is an issue of continual and sometimes heated debate, particularly when the state's largest mountain is involved.

Fair enough. But it should also be noted that exploratory skiing is woven deeply into the history and tradition of Stowe—and Vermont—skiing. I, for one, would feel the loss of something essential in the Stowe experience to see the door to that exploratory tradition slammed completely.

Even before the first trail (the Bruce) was cut in the winter of 1933-34, apostles of the relatively new sport of downhill skiing were prospecting about the mountain in search of possible routes of descent. It must have been a laborious undertaking. I try to imagine navigating through the trees on stiff, eight-foot skis made of hickory and without release bindings, and I feel a small shiver of respect.

Even when trails were cut, usually not much wider than your average garage door, the skiing was no piece of cake. After the Nose Dive was cut in 1935, its icy hairpin turns were enough to scare the daylights out of even the most accomplished skiers. Then along came the Front Four to further enhance the reputation for danger and adventure that skiing courted in its earlier years.

What we do today, on the advanced equipment now available, is by comparison child's play. At the same time, Stowe's terrain, taken as a whole, has probably mellowed somewhat over the years, thanks to extensive grooming and trail work that, among other things, have turned the once harrowing Nose Dive into a relatively smooth and tame descent. Stowe as a ski area is a bigger and more accomodating place now, and ambitious plans for the future are likely to make it even more so.

But I'd like to think that we are still tied in spirit—through the mountain's complexity and the constantly renewed challenges it throws at us—to the thrills those pioneers of the '30s must have experienced. I'd like to believe that what was true back in the '30s and true in the '60s when I made my first visit remains true today on newly defined terms: Stowe has a real and demonstrable right to call itself the Ski Capital of the East. ◨

With the colors of the fall foliage against the backdrop of early snow on Mt. Mansfield, Stowe is an image of idyllic perfection.

First There Was a Mountain

Such a deviously clever guy, that Ira Allen. Brother of Revolutionary War hero Ethan Allen and one of Vermont's founding fathers, Ira Allen stands out as a well-respected man in the annals of Vermont history. But as a real-estate broker he turned out to be something of a swindler, at least in the business of peddling Mt. Mansfield land.

When Vermont land was being divvied up among settlers in the middle part of the 18th century, Allen found himself owning the rights to several thousand acres in the now-defunct town of Mansfield, which included the mountain itself. At the time, Vermont was mostly wilderness, and it was not unusual for people to buy land they'd never seen. Allen had done just that, probably figuring that any 7,000-acre purchase had to be worth something. But when he began to survey it—reportedly becoming, in the process, the first white man to climb the mountain—he was not at all impressed with what he saw.

Ira Allen (left) was disappointed when he came to survey Mt. Mansfield in the late 18th century. The terrain, like Smugglers Notch (in the center, below), was rugged and unsuitable for farming. Buying the land, wrote Allen, gave friends "an opportunity to pass many hard jokes on me regarding my purchase." Opposite: As the logging industry grew, jury-rigged machines—such as the Snowtrax, a precursor to the snowmobile—hauled timber from the mountain to the mills.

The soil was rocky, and flat land suitable for crops and grazing was, not surprisingly, in very short supply. For agricultural purposes, Allen had himself a total loser. "At this point, I was owner of very near one third of the town [of Mansfield], and I could not discover lands that would make one good farm," was his glum report.

Almost immediately, then, he went about the business of trying to get rid of this worthless tract, and he was more than willing to resort to shadiness to get the job done. For starters, he misrepresented the quality of the mountain's timber, a pretty ordinary mix of hardwoods and conifers typical of a Vermont forest. The mountain, he claimed, was covered with rare "gumwood," a species of supposedly great value that existed only in the imagination of one Ira Allen.

Next, when prospective sellers of lots in Mansfield came to Allen, he offered to buy their land at a price higher than they might have expected. This gave the sellers pause. They figured Allen, who had surveyed the land, must know something that they (who had never seen their purchase) didn't. They fell for Allen's ruse, not only declining his offer to buy their land but buying his land on top of it. Allen was pretty pleased with his deceit, later indulging in what he called "a hearty laugh with my brothers."

As might have been expected, given the barrenness of the place, the town of Mansfield never amounted to much. Some of the earliest settlers had to make it through the winter on not much more than potatoes and salt, and even producing such meager foodstuff wasn't easy. One report tells of a farmer whose "potato patch was on such a steep sidehill that when he dug his

potatoes, he let them roll to the bottom and picked them up there." But at least the streams were full of healthy trout. One early settler wrote, perhaps a bit overenthusiastically, of catching "16 dozen in less than one hour, and they were large trout, too."

The population peaked in 1838 at 279 and then dwindled thereafter. By 1848 the town was effectively dissolved. Land that hadn't been annexed by Underhill, to the west of Mt. Mansfield, was absorbed by Stowe, to the east. That acquisition turned Stowe into Vermont's largest township in land area, a title it still claims.

So if you had come to Mt. Mansfield with farming in mind, you clearly had come to the wrong place. You might have made a modest go of logging, as a few companies managed to do through the 1800s. But Mt. Mansfield was hardly the ideal woodlot, either. The rocky soil, steep slopes, high elevation and

treeless summit were not the sort of environment in which to find big, healthy timber. In fact, the most significant profits to be made in Mt. Mansfield logging were in burning the wood to produce potash.

But Mt. Mansfield did have some intrinsic and lasting economic potential, and it took the grandiloquently named William Henry Harrison Bingham in the middle of the 1800s to realize it: The mountain was a tourist attraction. As Vermont's tallest mountain, with its clean mountain air and splendid views, Mansfield offered a welcome balm for lowland city folk. Bingham decided to make the most of it.

He may have drawn some local inspiration from Stillman Churchill, who in 1850 opened the Mansfield House, Stowe's first tourist inn (and now part of the Green Mountain Inn).

The Summit House

When William Henry Harrison Bingham built the Summit House atop Mt. Mansfield in 1858, he was at the vanguard of a trend that would spread throughout New England. At one time or another, hotels were built atop several mountains in Massachusetts and New Hampshire. And Bingham wasn't alone in Vermont in building a mountaintop hotel. At one time or another, lodging establishments would be built on Mt. Ascutney, Camel's Hump, Mt. Equinox, Killington, Mt. Lincoln and Snake Mountain.

In its heyday in the late 1800s, the Summit House was considered a glamorous place to stay. Its guest list included names like Roosevelt, Vanderbilt and Rothschild, and *Harper's* magazine in 1883 declared it a place for "discerning travelers."

Those travelers, drawn mainly by the mountain views and clean air, did not necessarily come because of elegant accommodations. The simple, wood-paneled walls, painted in white, were a far cry from the decor of a fancy city hotel, and the hotel was uninsulated.

Still, some semblance of urbanity was retained. In the dining room, for example, tables were covered in starched, white linens for a properly civilized meal. And an 1875 brochure advertised that "the table is always lavishly supplied and the house well kept in all respects and receives, as it well deserves, the best patronage of the intelligent and cultured seekers after health and recreation."

The earliest guests arrived at the hotel from town via stagecoach, which took them partway up the mountain, at which point they would finish the trip either by horseback or foot. When the Toll Road was soon extended all the way to the Summit House, guests could make the trip somewhat more comfortably, in horse-drawn carriages. The first automobile climbed the road in 1923.

The hotel in various forms survived for 107 years, although its popularity was at its zenith in the early years. In 1876, a total of 976 guests registered—a number that would never come close to being matched again. The hotel was condemned and razed in 1964, although guests had stopped coming in the late 1950s. By then the novelty of a mountaintop hotel had seen its day, and the expense and logistics of running the hotel as anything resembling a first-class operation—maintaining it and transporting food, personnel and guests—had become onerous.

Summer tourism in Stowe flourished long before skiing became popular. Many summer visitors would pack steamer trunks full of their best clothes and linens and stay in Stowe for a month or more. Stowe attracted some of America's wealthiest and most influential people, including Henry Ford (below, right).

Tourists were welcome, Churchill advertised, to come "for the purpose of enjoyment and rusticating in one of the pleasantest country villages in the state."

But if rusticating in a mountain village could be enjoyable, Bingham figured that rusticating in a mountaintop hotel was even more alluring. In quick order beginning in 1856, he had a small guesthouse (the Halfway House) built on the mountain, followed by a carriage road to the house, followed by the Summit House (see page 30) just below the Nose, with the road extended to reach the new hotel. By 1860, the Summit House was able to accommodate up to 10 guests, who would arrive by horse-drawn carriage. Among the hotel's attractions, according to promotional literature, was the promise of "absolutely no hay fever."

In many respects, Bingham was ahead of his time. In the 1850s, a handful of Boston-based intellectuals were heading to the Adirondacks for retreats known as "philosophers' camps." But for the most part, vacationing in the mountains of the Northeast didn't gain momentum until the turn of the century, when places like the Mt. Washington Hotel in New Hampshire and Lake Placid in the Adirondacks became popular. Perhaps because of a lack of competition, Stowe's summer tourism business soon began booming. In a town with a population of about 600 in the 1860s, the arrival of up to 500 summer visitors at a time was a virtual population explosion. In 1870, 1,000 people, traveling up the mountain on the Toll Road, visited the summit in one day. Some would go on foot; others would ride in horse-drawn carriages. Soon other inns would open, and Stowe was flatteringly referred to in some reports as "the Saratoga of Vermont."

The old Hotel.
Stowe Vt.

Bingham continued to have big ideas for developing Mt. Mansfield's tourist appeal. Among those that never materialized was a primitive cable car up the mountain. One of the more noteworthy schemes that did become a reality was the Mt. Mansfield Hotel in Stowe village. Known locally as the Big House or Big Hotel, it could accommodate as many as 600 guests in its 300 rooms, and it entertained them with a ballroom, bowling alley and park with a pond and rowboats. According to Stowe historian Ed Rhodes, some guests would reserve a year in advance in order to have custom multiroom suites built for them.

The hotel was short-lived, burning to the ground in 1889 (see page 191). But tourism would have no problem living on; Bingham had helped to bring to Stowe and Mt. Mansfield a cachet they would never lose.

While summer tourism on Mt. Mansfield thrived in the latter half of the 1800s, winter tourism lagged behind. It wasn't until the 1930s, as the new sport of downhill skiing began slowly to gain popularity in North America, that a few hardy pioneers began looking at the mountain with an eye toward developing a ski area. Mt. Mansfield seemed an obvious place to start. By New England standards, it represented something close to a ski-area ideal: the biggest mountain in Vermont with well over 2,000 skiable vertical feet on a continuous pitch.

Beyond its sheer size, Mt. Mansfield also featured a configuration especially suitable for skiing. The mountain's eastern facade formed a large, natural bowl, like a giant coliseum cut in half, capable both of capturing natural snowfall

and providing at least some protection from the wind. The rocky summit ridge provided an additional wind buffer, particularly against the frigid winds arriving ferociously from the west and northwest, when cold fronts gained gusto while moving over Lake Champlain before slamming into the Green Mountains.

Finally (and not insignificantly), Mt. Mansfield had aesthetic appeal. It was, as Bingham recognized, a handsome mountain in summer, but it could be even more so in winter. Its above-timberline summit—rare among Vermont's Green Mountains—turned a brilliant white with the snow and rime ice of winter. From the summit, the views were spectacular— east to New Hampshire's White Mountains and west, over Lake Champlain, to New York's Adirondacks.

Unfortunately, Mt. Mansfield's real-mountain appeal was mostly lost on the rare few who attempted to ski down the mountain before the first ski trails were cut in the 1930s. Craig Burt, a logging entrepreneur whose son would play a role in the development of downhill skiing a generation later, was one of the few who attempted any kind of downhill skiing at all in the Stowe area in the early 1900s.

"Around 1902 to 1905," Burt recalled years later, "a few of us took hardwood boards and bent up one end, nailed on a toe strap, and thought we were ready to ski… Control was at a minimum. Our skiing consisted of straight-running down a slope near the present school… However, 'spills without thrills' was not really skiing, and we soon lost interest."

The Green Mountair
From summit of Mt.

A view of the Summit House from Mt. Mansfield's Chin. One of the early visitors to the Summit House was Ralph Waldo Emerson, who, with his daughter Ellen, climbed the mountain from the Underhill side (the right side of the photo) after a lecture at Middlebury College in 1868.

If such small-hill skiing was unappealing, it's no wonder that the idea of skiing on Mt. Mansfield seemed all but ridiculous. Nevertheless, on February 1, 1914, a Dartmouth librarian named Nathaniel Goodrich thought he'd give it a try. It was a zany idea from the start. Goodrich, who had no skiing experience, was apparently inspired by nothing more than the whim of "trying something that had never been done before."

He'd heard stories about men who had climbed and skied the Mt. Washington Toll Road in New Hampshire, and an over-matched Goodrich was at least levelheaded enough to concede that that undertaking "seemed to a complete novice rather alarming." But Mt. Mansfield's Toll Road, snaking down the southeastern flank of the mountain from the summit, struck Goodrich as less intimidating and quite possibly doable for the confessed novice.

So after an arduous climb up the road, Goodrich began his descent in the company of a friend, Charles Blood, who came along on snowshoes. It was a good thing that Blood was there. Goodrich crashed often and had to be pulled out of the snow regularly. A run that today would take a few minutes took Goodrich about a half hour to complete.

Few would follow Goodrich's lead, and it's easy to understand why. Other than the Toll Road and a few scraggly logging trails, Mt. Mansfield's flanks were essentially an impenetrable forest. For prospective skiers without proper equipment or technique, the challenge presented by the terrain was beyond daunting. It was all but impossible.

An outing by a group of 10 Stowe-area locals on March 2, 1924, was further proof that skiing down the mountain in those

of Vermont.
ansfield.

P-234

days was far more trouble than it was worth. Scrambling up the Toll Road through the soft spring snow took the group four hours. The 10 were encumbered in their climb by nine-foot skis made of heavy ash slung over their shoulders.

By the time they arrived at the summit and had rested and lunched, the sun had moved west, and the snow on the shaded road had turned to ice. Four members of the group had never skied before, and unintended contact with trees was frequent in a descent that was probably more comical than it was dangerous. No wonder it would be another 10 years before interest in skiing Mt. Mansfield would really gain momentum.

Even then that optimal combination of terrain and aesthetics was not immediately apparent to Sepp Ruschp, an Austrian immigrant who arrived in Stowe in 1936 to found the first ski school on the mountain. Used to mountains of Alpine dimension, Ruschp took his first look at Mt. Mansfield and scratched his head in befuddlement. "I believe his comment was, 'Where's the mountain?'" says his son Peter Ruschp, who took over as Stowe's ski-school director many years later. "But then he climbed it and looked around and said, 'I can make this work.'"

Peter Ruschp, who can see Mt. Mansfield from his home on the Mountain Road, suggests now that his father might have underestimated the mountain when he first encountered it. While it might have lacked the sheer dimension of the mountains of Europe, says the younger Ruschp, it lacked none of the grandeur. "When you look out at Mt. Mansfield with that pinkish morning light on it," he says, "you get a feeling that it's a real mountain, that it's Alpine."

When Sepp Ruschp (right, in the Alps with son Peter; and skiing at Stowe, below) first saw Mt. Mansfield in 1936, he was unimpressed. "Where's the mountain?" Sepp reportedly asked.

❖

Geologically speaking, however, Mt. Mansfield is not half the Alp it used to be. Like the rest of the Green Mountains, Mt. Mansfield was the offspring of tectonic upthrust. Somewhere between 380 million and 500 million years ago, a sandy seabed was forced upward, and the combination of intense heat and pressure transformed the sand to rock.

As mountain infants those many million years ago, the Green Mountains probably looked more like the Himalayas or Rockies, all jagged peaks and rocky parapets, and much taller than they are now. But through eons of grinding, scarifying and polishing from erosion and glacial activity, what once were giants began gradually to take on the bearing of today's more low-slung, soft-shouldered mountains.

The last great ice age, ending about 12,000 years ago, was the most recent geomorphologic event to have had a significant hand in shaping the northern New England landscape. The entire countryside was engulfed in a sea of ice thousands of feet deep, and as the glaciers receded, mountains were reshaped, valleys were cut, and soils and rocks were deposited.

The result on Mt. Mansfield is a kind of crazy-quilt distribution of the mountain's component materials. So-called drift rocks and glacial erratics can be found all over the mountain. These sometimes very large chunks of rock were carried from afar by glacial movements and left in surroundings in which they have no geological connection. Many elements of the mountain soil, riding the glacial train, originated thousands of miles away. This, along with the mountain's latitude and elevation, helps

❖

Before an accurate survey in the 1920s, some thought Camel's Hump—actually 312 feet shorter than Mt. Mansfield—was Vermont's highest mountain.

explain why the summit ridge now hosts Vermont's largest community of Arctic tundra plants.

If you're looking for a precise explanation of the mountain's composition, turn to the wisdom of Elbridge C. Jacobs, Vermont's state geologist in the 1940s: "Mansfield's rocks are gneisses, schists and quartzites. Of these, the gneisses greatly predominate and are associated with the schist, while the quartzites lie below them....The sial grains are larger and secondary muscovite takes the place, to a large extent, of the scaly sericite. Megascopic garnets, delicate tourmalite needles, sizable fragments of ilmenite, magnetite and pyrite are seen."

Writing a few years later for the Vermont Geological Survey, Dr. Robert Christman was somewhat more comprehensible. Mt. Mansfield's rock, wrote Christman, "is a metamorphic rock which are [sic] formed by the recrystalization of older rocks under conditions of high temperature and pressure."

Take Jacobs' and Christman's scientific explanations for whatever they are worth, but in layman's terms, the point seems quite simple. Mansfield is a giant pile of rocks.

Still, it is a pretty impressive pile of rocks. When seen from the west, from the flat lands of the Lake Champlain basin, the mountain asserts its full, massive bulk. Its summit ridge runs more than two miles from north to south, and the full vertical relief of its western flank, from the lake level to the ridge, is 4,189 feet.

Yet it is the mountain's eastern facade, the Stowe side of the mountain, that seems to have won more interest from human beings over the years. Part of that undoubtedly has to do with the fact that the western slope of the mountain rises more abruptly

The features of the mountain's ridgeline form the approximate profile of a human face. From left to right (with some imagination required): the Forehead, Nose, Lip, Chin, and Adam's Apple.

and is less hospitable, whereas the wind-sheltered eastern side, with that natural bowl configuration like two hands cupped open in greeting, seems somehow more inviting.

Perspective from the east also provides perhaps the better view of Mansfield's best-known feature—the approximate profile of a human face formed from the features along the summit ridge. To see the profile might require exercising a good deal of imagination, but then that's something people living in mountainous areas have been doing for centuries. Blessed with either great visualization or too much time on their hands, they look for shapes in the mountains surrounding them: animals, ships at sea, prehistoric creatures, pieces of furniture, stacks of books and, above all, parts of the human anatomy.

Abanaki natives originally called Mt. Mansfield Mozeo-de-

be-wadso, meaning Mountain with a Head like a Moose. It is not precisely known when the more widely accepted interpretation of the mountain ridge as a human facial profile took root, although it, too, probably has its origins in native lore. According to one Native American myth, after a chief died on the summit during a terrible storm, his after-life spirit rearranged the ridgeline in the shape of his face.

By turning your head sidewise, you can see the elongated facial features—forehead, nose, lip, chin and Adam's apple—as the ridge runs from south to north. Those with a particularly vivid imagination claim that there is also a nostril (a cave below the Nose) and an eyebrow.

The profile is not, at least by the standards of some snobs and chauvinists, indicative of higher intelligence or breeding. As one

The First Stowe Winter Carnival

Before 1921 in Stowe, outdoor winter recreation was essentially considered the province of children and crazy folk. The common thinking was, who, of sound mind, would want to spend any more time than necessary outside in the cold and snow?

One of the crazies was Craig Burt, an ardent winter enthusiast who was one of the first people in the Stowe area to try skiing (shortly after the turn of the century). In 1921, Burt and a handful of other enthusiasts, under the aegis of the Stowe Civic Club, decided to try shaking the community out of its winter lethargy. So they set about organizing the first Stowe Winter Carnival, a seminal event in the development of winter tourism in Stowe. It was an event, Burt wrote later, "this community had to have in order to overcome the inertia of the large number of people who looked on the out-of-doors in winter as something to be endured."

On February 8, 1921, the action got under way: obstacle races, snowshoeing, tobogganing, skijoring, skating and ski jumping. To raise money to pay for the carnival, a minstrel show was staged, apparently with considerable success; the total take was $1,000. Between 1,000 and 2,000 people attended the four-day festival, but the real crowd pleaser was the jumping. According to Carrie Slayton, a Moscow resident writing many years later, "Everyone was very excited about the games and races, but the ski jumping seemed to have impressed them the most, and all wanted skis right away."

The carnival survives today, but only after having been revived in the mid 1970s, after a long hiatus. It has become a nine-day affair, with a much longer roster of events than the original. The carnival now includes a citizens' super G race, cross-country racing, snowshoe racing, an ice-sculpting competition, beer tasting, snow golf and a "wintermeister" competition combining downhill skiing, cross-country skiing and speed skating. But the impetus behind the carnival now is the same as it was in 1921: to roust the local, sometimes sedentary citizenry out of its mid-winter doldrums.

observer wrote in 1857, "Mansfield's forehead is not very intellectual—his chin, like that of many others, being the highest. He has a regular cave of a mouth, terribly twisted, which opens down on the northeast side, yawning and aweful, with a breath that strikes a blight like that of winter." The Nose, wrote another observer a few years later, was "a right Yankee sneezer, 300 feet high." This was not, presumably, meant to be a compliment.

Mt. Mansfield's anthropomorphic ridgeline might be the mountain's best-known feature, but it is not the only feature of note. One particular curiosity is Cantilever Rock, on the mountain's western flank, which extends almost 30 feet straight out from the mountainside. Geologists seem at a loss in trying to produce a satisfactory explanation for the presence of this giant granite finger, wedged between rock cliffs above and below.

Other features of the mountain are perhaps most notable for their resonant names: the Rock of Terror, the Cave of the Winds and the Lake of the Clouds.

But if you were to single out Mt. Mansfield's most noteworthy feature, you'd most likely turn to Smugglers' Notch, the steep-walled passage between Mansfield's northeastern shoulder and neighboring Sterling Peak. With cliffs rising 1,000 feet on either side, the notch is a testament to the sort of natural artwork that thousands of years of sculpting erosion and glacial might are capable of. The notch shows itself to particularly dramatic effect in winter when the cliffs become decorated with bands of ice and new snow, and after a summer rain, when instantaneous and short-lived waterfalls appear like filigree on the rock.

It is a storied place as much as it is a handsome place, having

SMUGGLERS' NOTCH
Forbidden Trade with Canada
passed through here, 1808-14

The Notch gained its name after
Jefferson's Embargo Acts of 1808
and the War of 1812, when cattle
were driven north and Canadian
goods were smuggled into New
England through this picturesque
gap beside majestic Mt. Mansfield,
remote from revenue officers.
VERMONT HISTORIC SITES COMMISSION

In Smuggler's Notch

Traveling through Smugglers Notch (below) in the 1800s was rugged. When the road through the Notch was improved in 1922, it became a route for smuggling liquor from Canada during Prohibition.

hosted a long-running game of hide-and-seek over the years. The notch earned its name in the years following the passage of the Embargo Act of 1807, which prohibited trade with Britain during growing hostilities that eventually led to the War of 1812.

In January 1809, Congress extended the law to make trade with Canada, then under British rule, also illegal—a big economic hit for Vermonters who relied on commerce with their northern neighbors. The simple solution: break the law. The embargo only spurred a small industry in contraband goods traded between Vermont and Canada, and if the smugglers needed a place to hide the loot—including such hard-to-hide goods as cattle—the narrow passageway and small caves of the notch were about as good a place as any.

Later, the notch served as a hiding place for fugitive slaves on their way to Canada during the Civil War and finally for liquor smuggled in from Canada during Prohibition in the '20s. There are those in town who will try to convince you that there are still bottles of prime 80-year-old booze to be found in caves in the notch, though this most likely is the kind of bogus information locals enjoy passing on to gullible tourists.

Mt. Mansfield is Vermont's tallest mountain, but it hasn't always been obviously so. Over the years, as its reported size would grow and shrink, the mountain was periodically denied its rightful claim to being Vermont's high point. Hypsometry, the science of measuring elevations, has not always been precise, and at times regional rivalries took advantage of the imprecision of mountain measurement to indulge in a little self-promotional spin.

The Whip

Known officially as the Whip Bar & Grill in the Green Mountain Inn, the Whip draws its name from a prominent feature of its decor—four dozen whips, vertically aligned as a partition between the bar and a seating area. The whips come in varying lengths and with varying leather-making details, bearing varying signs of wear that speak of a storied past. All are relics of a previous era, when horse-drawn carriages were the main means of transportation by which tourists traveled around Stowe.

In fact, carriage travel was so prevalent in the

mid 1800s that one of Stowe's most prominent structures was an enormous barn, the Livery, built to house horses and carriages for guests of the Mt. Mansfield Hotel. When the barn was torn down in 1953, the proprietors of the Green Mountain Inn had the good sense to salvage some of its beams, now also part of the Whip.

While Mt. Mansfield was by consensus considered Vermont's high point through most of the 1800s, surveying work by the U.S. Coast and Geodetic Survey (USCGS) in the 1890s cast doubt on the validity of that assertion. The USCGS survey suggested, somewhat ambiguously, that Killington and even Camel's Hump, a few miles south of Stowe, were higher than Mt. Mansfield.

Armed with this information the *Rutland News*, perhaps seeking to bring some elite distinction to otherwise blue-collar central Vermont, took the opportunity to lay it on its northern neighbor. "Mt. Mansfield," the *News* declared, "has been standing many years under false pretenses."

Such bravado proved to be relatively short-lived. In 1924 the U.S. Geological Survey began exhaustively and more accurately surveying Vermont, restoring, in the process, Mt. Mansfield to its rightful preeminence. The mountain's height was set at 4,393 feet, although even that supposedly official measurement was apparently not completely on the mark. In recent years, the mountain's actual height has been recalculated to be 4,395 feet. Killington ranks second at 4,235 feet, while 4,083-foot Camel's Hump falls all the way to fourth, just behind 4,135-foot Mt. Ellen.

Although Mansfield might be Vermont's tallest mountain, it may not be the snowiest. For many years, that distinction has been claimed by Jay Peak, the northernmost mountain in the main spine of the Green Mountains. In the record winter of 2000-01, for example, some 571 inches of snow fell on Jay Peak, according to the resort. In that same year, 388 inches were independently recorded on Mansfield. That's well above Mansfield's average annual snowfall of about 260 inches, but a total snowfall of more than 300 inches a year is not uncommon.

Snow comes early to Mt. Mansfield and lasts long, sometimes impressively so. On October 10, 1925, for example, more than two feet of snow fell on the Toll Road. Drifts were five feet deep. Five elderly guests stranded at the Summit House hotel had to be rescued by a sledge drawn by a four-horse team. They abandoned the Cadillac that they had driven up to the hotel, but not the cow that provided milk for the hotel; the cow trudged

An average of 260 inches of snow falls annually on Mt. Mansfield. Big storm cycles aren't uncommon; in the epic winter of 1970-1971, almost seven feet of snow fell in the month of December alone.

along behind the sledge as it made its way down the road.

Such powerful October storms are unusual, but spring storms aren't. In fact, March is the snowiest month on Mansfield, and April often isn't far behind. In 1996, for example, a total of 86 inches of snow—more than seven feet—fell on the mountain after April 1. So while Jay might be snowier, Mansfield's snowfall statistics are nothing to sneeze at.

In fact, Jay's snowfall is usually considered a meteorological aberration for Vermont. Mansfield's snowfall, on the other hand, is considered something close to the semi-official snowfall for the state. Since 1954, the University of Vermont (and subsequently Burlington television station WCAX-TV) has maintained a snow-measuring stake on the mountain at 3,950 feet near the Toll Road. Never mind that the snow depth at the stake—on a moun-

tain, at high elevation—has almost nothing to do with snow depths regularly encountered by valley-dwelling Vermonters. That fact doesn't deter radio and television meteorologists from reporting, in their daily broadcast, the depth at the 12-foot stake as if it were the state's gold standard of snow measurement.

Add, then, to Mt. Mansfield's size, configuration and aesthetic appeal the fact that it is also something of a snow magnet, and you can easily understand why the early skiing pioneers, looking to create a ski area, were drawn to the mountain as if to some irresistible force field. They would converge on the mountain from three fronts: from New York, from Europe and from Stowe itself. Within a brief few years in the 1930s, Mt. Mansfield would become the centerpiece in what had arguably become the most popular ski destination in America. ⌧

Civilian Conservation Corps workers assembled for the first day of cutting the first trail on Mt. Mansfield in 1933. The federal program–designed to put 500,000 unemployed people to work–required enrollees to be between 18 and 25 years old and unmarried.

CHAPTER 2

Back to the Beginning

Because the initial idea of a ski area in Stowe began to take shape on several fronts, who can say exactly where and when the first seed was planted? Perhaps as good a place as any to start is a sloping pasture near Hillsdale, New York, in the winter of 1931.

Roland Palmedo, a New York City securities specialist, was in Hillsdale indulging in the relatively nouveau sport of downhill skiing. It was an outing that might ordinarily have escaped historical notice, and even the fact that Palmedo broke his leg that day might seem to deserve little more than a tiny footnote in medical annals. But that injury helped set in motion a kind of domino effect: a chain of events that would soon lead to the founding of a ski area on Mt. Mansfield.

In 1931, downhill skiing was a virtual nonentity in America, a marginal activity practiced only by a handful of hardy outdoorsmen and eccentrics. "Skiing"

Left: A skilled pilot, Roland Palmedo flew around New England in an open-cockpit plane to scout out promising mountains for a ski area. Opposite: the country's first rope tow was installed in Woodstock, Vermont in 1934, three years before the first tow came to Stowe. The Woodstock tow used a Model-T engine to drive 1,800 feet of rope.

in 1931 generally meant either cross-country skiing or ski jumping, a highly popular competitive sport at the time. There was no such thing as a legitimate ski area anywhere in the country, and the world's first rope tow wouldn't arrive on the scene until three years later, in Woodstock, Vermont. If you wanted to ski, you made do with whatever snow-covered hillside you could find. You also had to make do with the most rudimentary of equipment—most likely inflexible, eight-foot skis made of hickory or ash.

Exactly what gear Palmedo was using on that day in 1931 is no longer a matter of record. Even how he got to Hillsdale is no longer known, although as a former World War I aviator, Palmedo would often strap his skis to the side of an open-cock-pit plane and fly himself to skiing locations he thought especially

promising. What is known, however, is that he didn't acquit himself particularly well, and his broken leg brought on the prospect of a rehabilitation period of several months.

What is also known is that Roland Palmedo was not a guy who took lying down easily. "He certainly had a lot of energy, both physical and mental," recalls Ken Quackenbush, who in the 1950s and 1960s managed Mad River Glen, a ski area south of Stowe, for Palmedo. Palmedo's interest in skiing was born from a seemingly limitless vigor that drove him to become a dedicated kayaker, mountain climber, golfer and tennis player. Such was his restlessness that, as a National Guardsman training in Vermont in the 1920s, he would hike up Mt. Mansfield as a way of passing his R and R time. Taking time off simply to take time off was not something that came easily to Palmedo.

The ski injury was a temporary and annoying wrench in the works. It is easy to envision Palmedo in his Upper East Side apartment stewing away, like a racehorse restricted to his stall. "I had to find something to occupy my time," he said, and that "something" turned out to be poring over U.S. Geological Survey (USGS) maps of New England. Palmedo became obsessed with what could fairly be considered a completely out-of-the-box idea at the time: finding the ideal place in the Northeast to go downhill skiing.

Having visited the Alps in the late 1920s, where downhill skiing was developing rapidly, he had some idea of what he was looking for. "He'd seen a lot of what skiing had already become in Europe, and he had ideas," says Quackenbush. "He could see his own picture." That picture began to crystallize through studying USGS maps with an eye for a mountain with the right combination of size, pitch, location and, perhaps, logging trails to be used as rudimentary ski trails. New England mountains might not have the breathtaking dimensions of the Alps, but they still held several promising possibilities. The best of the bunch, the hobbled Palmedo decided after due consideration, was Mt. Mansfield.

Fully recovered a year later, Palmedo convinced a New York friend, Jose Machado, to join him on a Washington's Birthday trip north to investigate the mountain he had singled out. The two rode by train from Manhattan to Waterbury, Vermont, then by a trolley from Waterbury north to Stowe. (That was the last year the trolley, built in 1883 and powered by electricity, would run. Such was its extravagant power consumption,

Before any ski trails were cut, the Toll Road (below) was the main route both up and down the mountain. But serious skiers didn't consider the road a real skiing challenge.

TOLL ROAD
MT. MANSFIELD
STOWE, VT.

according to Waterbury-based ski-area historian Brian Lindner, that "house lights would dim when the trolley began climbing Shutesville Hill.")

In Stowe, Palmedo and Machado befriended a local logging entrepreneur named Franklin Griffin, one among a handful of Stowe locals who were also beginning to ponder the possibilities of downhill skiing on Mt. Mansfield. Griffin agreed to drive the two New Yorkers up the Mountain Road. Or at least he agreed to go as far as the road had been plowed—about to where today's Matterhorn pub is located and about a mile from the beginning of the Toll Road the New Yorkers planned to climb. In 1932, few people in Stowe had much use for Mt. Mansfield in winter, and plowing the road for the full five miles from town to the mountain made little sense.

Palmedo and Machado hiked up the snow-covered Toll Road, which wound up the mountain's southeastern flank. They surveyed the mountain's eastern facade, with its multiple variations in pitch and considerable vertical drop, and they apparently liked what they saw. Here was a mountain with ideal skiing terrain, both in size and variation, and it was just a few miles from an attractive Vermont town that was easily accessible from New York.

Upon returning to the city, Palmedo began to stir up interest in Stowe skiing among members of the New York Amateur Ski Club. In the club's *Ski Bulletin,* he wrote: "Stowe is in northern Vermont, 10 miles north of Waterbury, which latter is on the main line of the Central Vermont Railroad and from which an electric trolley runs to Stowe... The hills on all sides are said to

Trained as an engineer, Charlie Lord had a keen eye for making the most of the contours of Mt. Mansfield's terrain.

have numerous logging roads suitable for skiing…" Club members, mostly well-to-do New Yorkers, were apparently sold. By the next winter they began riding the train north in significant numbers, to discover for themselves this magical place that Palmedo was promoting.

It would be a historical misrepresentation to suggest that Roland Palmedo alone was the genius behind the birthing of Stowe as a ski resort. But in 1932, he provided a critical link: the connection between a potential ski area (Stowe) and potential skiers in the members of the New York Amateur Ski Club. He also managed to convince New York companies like Saks Fifth Avenue to sponsor extra cars for the weekend winter trains between New York and Vermont—the Skimeister trains as they would come to be called.

With that swell of interest, other elements in the genesis of a ski area began to fall into place—trails, lodges, a ski school and, by 1940, the longest chairlift in the world at the time. Stowe, the ski area, was on its way, and while Palmedo played an instrumental role, it certainly wasn't all his doing. When it came to the actual physical work of turning the idea of a ski area into a reality, a handful of Stowe locals would do most of the work.

Charlie Lord was a highway engineer working in Montpelier for the state of Vermont at the time Palmedo came to check out Mt. Mansfield. He was also a dedicated skier, and when it would come to laying out a ski area, the combination of a skier's passion and an engineer's acuity would serve him well. As the historian Brian Lindner describes him, "Charlie was a silent genius, excep-

Opposite: Charlie Lord, on one of many ski trips through northern New England, skiing Bear Mountain in New Hampshire in 1933. Lord's frequent skiing companion was Ab Coleman (top, left, and above left, with Lord, all on Mt. Mansfield in 1938).

tionally low-keyed. But as an engineer, he had an incredible knack for designing ski trails." If Palmedo brought people into the equation of creating a ski area in Stowe, Lord would bring saws, axes, an engineer's sensibilities and raw, trail-building manpower.

Lord and his regular skiing partner, Abner Coleman, were among the rare few adventurers exploring the mountains of northern Vermont on skis in the early 1930s. They availed themselves of the cutting-edge ski technology of the time: relatively short seven-foot skis for extra maneuverability and metal toe irons rather than the leather toe straps more commonly used at that time. They were practitioners of the so-called Zdarsky technique in which a single long pole was swung back and forth in front of the body and dragged in the snow, both for speed control and turning leverage.

That indulgence took Lord, Coleman and others all over the mountains of northern New England. They traveled east to Burke Mountain and Berlin; south to Warren, Bolton and Camel's Hump; and east to Cabot. They were hunting for all things skiable—a trail, an open slope, anything with enough pitch to allow them to glide downhill and with enough openness to keep the interference of trees to a minimum. They journeyed to New Hampshire to ski Mt. Washington's Tuckerman Ravine, and they stayed at home to ski Mt. Mansfield. And somewhere in all of their gadding about, an idea germinated in Lord's mind: If downhill skiing was to be enjoyed fully in Vermont, trails would need to be cut. Mt. Mansfield, Vermont's biggest mountain, seemed a logical place to start.

In 1932, in the full grip of the Depression, Lord was laid off

from his job. His economic well-being might have suffered a temporary setback, but he had no problem figuring out what to do with his newly found spare time. "Being a gentleman of leisure," he wrote in his diary in the winter of 1932-33, "more skiing was indulged."

Fortuitously for Lord during his stint working for the state, he had befriended Perry Merrill, the man in charge of Vermont's state forestry department. Merrill had studied forestry in Sweden, where he'd seen cross-country trails cut through the woods. He'd also been keeping an eye on a ski-trail movement that in the early 1930s was already afoot in neighboring New Hampshire.

So cutting ski trails on Mt. Mansfield didn't strike Merrill as an oddball idea, especially as a way of promoting more public use of state forests. Guided by Roland Palmedo's urging, winter vis-

itors were now on the increase in Vermont. Better ski trails could only encourage visitation, a potential boon for an economically beleaguered state.

When Merrill petitioned the state government to back his trail-building scheme, however, he ran into stiff resistance. Vermont legislators were less than enthusiastic about siphoning away money from a cash-strapped state budget for something so frivolous as skiing. They did not, apparently and understandably, savor the prospect of explaining to their constituents that money for such necessities as road improvement or rural electrification had been diverted to building ski trails for the entertainment of a bunch of rich New Yorkers.

Merrill would have to go elsewhere to find the necessary funds, and the federal Civilian Conservation Corps (CCC)

Opposite: Charlie Lord with a CCC crew during a lunch break. What the crew lacked in trail-clearing machinery, they made up for in manpower. Above: Some CCC workers were based in Ranch Camp, which later would become Stowe's first "ski-in, ski-out" lodge in the 1930s.

proved to be his godsend. Created in March 1933 by an act of Congress, the CCC was assigned to building roads, lodges, campgrounds and trails throughout the country as a way of putting the unemployed back to work. Cutting ski trails was a job right up the CCC's alley. In fact, CCC teams had already begun doing just that in New Hampshire.

Under Merrill's urging, Lord was hired to lead a Waterburybased CCC team to cut ski trails on Mt. Mansfield. (Even this irked some legislators, who felt that the CCC manpower could be put to better use. But the CCC was a federal program, and the Vermonters could do little more than breathe fire and voice their disenchantment.)

The trail cutting was an ad hoc project by any assessment. No scientific survey of the mountain was taken; Lord simply eye-

balled the terrain, made a few rough sketches and put his 20-man team to work in November 1933. Using axes and two-man crosscut saws, the team labored through the deepening snow, cutting a trail 10 to 20 feet wide.

"We didn't have any great knowledge, or written plans, or books to guide us," Lord explained many years later. "It was trial and error. We had to avoid swamps, wet spots, boulders, dropoffs, and that accounts for the trail being quite twisted and rugged." In short, the job wasn't easy. But as Lord said, "We had lots of manpower, and if you have enough manpower, you could do anything."

"Anything" turned out to be a trail beginning at the Toll Road summit and descending for four miles down the mountain's southeastern shoulder, covering 2,250 vertical feet. It was a trail

that came in three parts: the first third on an expert pitch reaching 30 degrees; the second third, intermediate; and the final stretch, novice. Its terminus was Ranch Camp (see page 58), a logging camp converted into a guest camp for skiers by its owner and proprietor, Craig O. Burt.

That first trail, completed by the spring of 1934, was named the Bruce Trail, in honor of a Stowe lumberman named H.M. Bruce. No surprise there—the only people to spend much time on the mountain in winter before the CCC crew arrived were loggers. A second trail, designed as an easier alternative to the Bruce Trail, was cut from about three quarters of the way down the Toll Road. In all, the initial phase of trail cutting took about six months.

The Bruce Trail will go down in history as the first ski trail

cut on Mt. Mansfield, but it didn't prove to be the trail that really launched Stowe skiing. In the summer of 1935, Lord and his crew began work on a trail that would descend from the Nose of Mt. Mansfield toward Barnes Camp, another converted logging camp near the mouth of Smugglers' Notch. Lord originally intended to name the trail the Barnes Trail, after the camp. But when the trail was rerouted to end not at the camp but at a nearby parking lot (another CCC project), a new name had to be conceived.

Perry Merrill struck upon the obvious. The trail began at the Nose and dropped 2,500 vertical feet in about two miles, pretty precipitous going for a trail in those days. It was described by Lord as "a very fast, steep trail for experienced runners only." A fast, steep trail from the Nose—why not call it Nose Dive?

Almost immediately, the Nose Dive took its place alongside the Thunderbolt Trail on Mt. Greylock in the Berkshires and the Taft Slalom Trail on Cannon Mountain in New Hampshire as one of the preeminent race trails in American skiing. It was particularly famous—or infamous—for its first quarter mile or so, comprising seven hellishly zigzagging turns. The turns were less the result of diabolical design than necessity; the work was all done by hand. "We had to avoid ledges and drop-offs," Lord explained many years later. "That was how we came up with seven turns on the Nose Dive."

In 1936, the CCC crew also finished construction of the Stone Hut, the first warming hut on the mountain for skiers. A CCC-built base lodge would follow a few years later. The basics of a legitimate ski area—trails, warming hut, parking lot—were falling into place. More trails would continue to be cut: Chin Clip and Merrill in the area that the modern-day gondola now services; S-53 and Lord, descending from the Nose area; Tear Drop, descending down the west side of the mountain toward Underhill; and so on. And thanks largely to Roland Palmedo, interest in skiing at Stowe was spreading rapidly in New York, New Haven, Hartford and other cities along the train route from New York to Vermont. The skiers were coming, and a ski area—or at least the scaffolding of one—was there to greet them.

The Stowe community couldn't help but take notice. Tourism had for decades been a staple of the area's summer economy. Winter, on the other hand, was a tourism black hole. Most of the town's inns and lodges simply shuttered up in winter,

Ranch Camp

"A trip with the team back into the head of the Ranch Valley is something to treasure. Up a winding trail over which millions of feet of logs were once hauled, you are carried into the valley. Mt. Dewey lies impressively on your left, the Forehead of Mt. Mansfield on your right, while the sled creaks over the frosty snow."

In the December 1941 edition of the Ranch Camp newsletter, David Burt (of the notable Stowe logging family) wrote of the soul-soothing tranquility of the trip, by horse-drawn sledge, in to Ranch Camp. In the 1930s—in the earliest years of Stowe skiing, when the only way to get up Mt. Mansfield was to hike—Ranch Camp was a skiers' haven right out of the imagery of Robert Frost. Sequestered deep in the woods and snow of the Ranch Valley, the former logging camp offered a

welcome escape into rusticity for skiers, most of whom were leaving behind the hectic pace of city life. At the end of the Bruce Trail (the first cut on Mt. Mansfield), the camp was in a convenient location for skiers who wanted to start early on their hike up the mountain.

The camp consisted of not much more than shed-like bunkhouses and a cookhouse with its own bunkroom. The cookhouse was heated by a stove made of two 55-gallon steel drums, while the cooking was done on a cast-iron stove. Depending on the severity of the winter, as many as 40 cords of wood might be burned. The camp did have its own electricity generator, although kerosene lanterns were on hand for the occasions when the balky generator failed.

Food and luggage were brought in by horse-drawn wagon, sleigh or sledge, depending on the snow conditions. The driver, a true-Vermont farmer named Neil Robinson, became something of a Ranch Camp celebrity, known, as one Ranch Camper wrote, for "his jovial twinkle and dry humor." While Robinson hauled in luggage, most of the camp guests would ski the one-mile route to the camp from the Mountain Road. Trim Conkling, who managed the camp for three years in the late 1930s, described the procession in a 1977 article in *SKIING* magazine: "Perhaps 30 or 35 skiers would pole along in the dark. We often carried red flares that weirdly illuminated the snow, the trees, and the ice-choked Ranch Brook."

The camp was able to accommodate up to 50 overnight guests, and even if the lodging arrangements were tight and inelegant, the price was certainly right. In 1936, according to Charlie Lord, lodging rates were set at between $1 and $1.25, with meals an extra $1 a day. With the camp's increase in popularity, prices soared—all the way to $2.50 to $3.50 a day for bed and board.

The construction of Stowe's single chairlift in 1940 signaled the beginning of the end for Ranch Camp. The lift ascended the northeast flank of Mt. Mansfield beneath the Nose, shifting the focus of skiing away from the Ranch Valley. The camp is now long gone, but its sylvan environment today remains much as it was during the camp's heyday—heavily wooded with streams running through it, the tranquility disturbed only by the occasional backcountry skier.

Members of the Mt. Mansfield Ski Club in 1937. Originally the Stowe Ski Club, the club was reorganized under its new name in 1933 with new priorities focused on downhill skiing on Mt. Mansfield. The club is still active today.

because who in their right mind would want to come visit Vermont in the cold and snow? Now, with this crazy new sport of downhill skiing picking up steam, winter began to look a lot more promising.

One of those who got an early whiff of skiing's economic promise was Craig Burt, Sr. In 1932, Burt converted his logging camp in the Ranch Valley, at the southeastern edge of Mt. Mansfield, into a facility to house winter guests. The tariff was $2 a night per person, breakfast included.

His Ranch Camp might have lacked elegant hotel amenities, but it had the big advantage of being close to the mountain and the skiing. In fact, its backwoods rusticity turned out to be a drawing card for many of the city people, and by the winter of 1934, when a total of 544 guests were registered, the camp had

become, in its own small way, a smashing success. Ranch Camp made a clear statement: Winter recreation, downhill skiing specifically, could be an attraction to out-of-state visitors. One by one, inn and lodge proprietors in Stowe began pulling back the shutters and jumping on the winter bandwagon.

A cultural clash was probably inevitable between the visitors—who, like Palmedo, were mostly wealthy city people—and the local Stowe folk. But the visitors brought money and international recognition to Stowe, and a shared passion for skiing no doubt engendered a mutual respect. As Abner Coleman wrote in 1954 in a letter to a friend: "Although we natives often resented them, I feel now that the Amateur Ski Club of New York, led by Roland Palmedo, did as much as any group to make Mt. Mansfield known to the rest of the world."

Sepp Ruschp (above, left) introduced the Arlberg technique of skiing–pioneered by the famed Austrian ski instructor Hannes Schneider–to Stowe skiers in the 1930s.

In December 1933, Burt and Griffin, along with other local skiing enthusiasts, formed the Mt. Mansfield Ski Club, a direct offspring of the preexisting Stowe Ski Club. The titular repositioning of the club was symbolic: Downhill skiing on the mountain, not cross-country skiing in and around town, was now where the action was.

The general objectives of the club, Griffin (the club's president) wrote, were "the provision, improvement and maintenance in the Mt. Mansfield region of facilities contributing to the skiing enjoyment of its members, and also to aid all skiers in obtaining the greatest amount of pleasure while visiting this section of Vermont." If the "greatest amount of pleasure" was to be derived, however, it soon became apparent to the club chieftains that somebody would have to teach the skiers how to ski.

In the mid '30s, most of those who came to Stowe to try the newfangled sport of downhill skiing were absolute neophytes. You couldn't just send them out on their own onto a trail like the Nose Dive; they'd kill themselves. But who could teach them proper technique? The best instructors in the world were in Europe, not in Stowe.

As Griffin and company pondered their options, a letter arrived in the spring of 1936 from across the Atlantic. A young Austrian was inquiring about the possibility of setting up a ski school in Stowe. Might the Mt. Mansfield Ski Club be interested in his services? The Austrian's name was Sepp Ruschp.

Ruschp, a native of Linz, was certainly qualified for the job. An engineer by trade, he was a skier through and through, a winner of national championships in Austria in cross-country,

Birth of the Ski Patrol

Despite its rich and long skiing tradition, Stowe can claim relatively few firsts. The first trails, the first tow, the first chairlift, the first race—all can be traced to other parts of the country. But in 1934, Stowe skiers made what is arguably one of the most valuable contributions to U.S. skiing by organizing the country's first ski patrol.

The original idea was Roland Palmedo's, who had traveled to Europe and observed a Swiss Army ski patrol, the Parsenndienst, near Davos. Palmedo suggested to Frank Griffin, president of the Mt. Mansfield Ski Club, that a similar patrol ought to be started up at Stowe. A steady stream of skiers, or at least those who imagined themselves to be skiers, were beginning to arrive by train from New York and other cities to the south. They knew little about skiing and even less about the trails on Mt. Mansfield. They would need help, Palmedo said to Griffin, in safely navigating the mountain.

The first patrollers, who went into action in the winter of 1934–35, were primarily guides and hosts; they stationed themselves on the mountain to keep visitors from getting lost in an era before trails were neatly cut and clearly marked. They also gave skiers advice on what wax to use. The wood-based skis of the era had to be waxed regularly—sometimes for every run—and any waxing mistake could make for a miserable run.

As the number of skiers increased, however, the number of accidents grew. It became clear to the patrol leaders that providing assistance to the injured would have to become the principal focus of their efforts.

Patrollers were required to take a Red Cross course in rescue and first aid. Toboggans made of corrugated roofing material were stationed at strategic spots on the mountain, with blankets and emergency medical supplies. By the time the U.S. Eastern Amateur Ski Association Championships arrived in Stowe in 1937, a well-organized system was in place, and visiting ski enthusiasts took notice.

They took notice, too, at the National Championships held the next year at Stowe. Roger Langley, president of the National Ski Association, was especially impressed. He said as much to C. Minot "Minnie" Dole during the races, and the wheels of action were set in motion. Dole, whose good friend Frank Edson had died of a punctured lung in a skiing accident two years earlier, was particularly keen on promoting safety and rescue. Urged on by Langley and inspired by the Mt. Mansfield Ski Patrol, Dole would go on to found the National Ski Patrol (NSP).

Over the years, the National Ski Patrol became the principal force in spreading the gospel of safety, first aid and rescue to ski areas across the country. Over time, however, its influence—as primarily a volunteer organization—would fade as ski areas began to hire and train their own full-time professional patrollers. Today, the National Ski Patrol has about 28,000 members. They are divided into volunteer and professional divisions and serve at hundreds of ski resorts around the country.

Left: C. Minot "Minnie" Dole was inspired by Stowe's ski patrol and subsequently founded the National Ski Patrol (NSP). Dole was also the driving force behind the foundation of the famed 10th Mountain Division during World War II. Opposite: Stowe's first rope tow, installed in 1937 in the Toll House area. A season's pass cost $5. Extensive trail clearing would soon follow.

❖

downhill and slalom. He had had some experience in Austria in ski instruction. And, according to his son Peter, "he was full of energy and passion. He was an apostle for skiing."

In 1936, ski teaching in Europe was becoming ominously tinged with growing concerns about war. To Sepp, America seemed both safer and more promising. "He could see what was happening in Europe," says Peter Ruschp. "The storm clouds [of war] were readily apparent. But also, the U.S. was the place people wanted to go. Skiing was in its infancy, and there were opportunities." According to Sepp's own calculations, there were more than 600 ski instructors in Austria, whereas in America the field was essentially wide open.

Sepp sent more than 50 letters to ski clubs in the United States and received four encouraging replies. An offer from

Yellowstone National Park intrigued him, but he decided that he would do better by signing on with the Mt. Mansfield Ski Club. Exactly why Ruschp came to that decision isn't altogether clear, for the ski club's offer was by no means lucrative. The pay was $100 a month, with the club also offering a 50 percent cut of anything over $100 a month in club revenues, which at the time were pretty meager.

When he arrived in Stowe on December 10, 1936, Ruschp had further reason to question the wisdom of his choice. The weather was unseasonably warm, there was almost no snow, and Mt. Mansfield appeared depressingly puny compared with the Alps he was familiar with. It appeared that he had little to work with: no more than a handful of trails, no lifts and only a four-month season, meaning in theory that he

❖

would be in a foreign country for eight months of the year without gainful employment.

But he hiked up the mountain, took an apparently pleasing run in powder snow down the Nose Dive, and became encouraged. "I looked [at] a map," he told a *SKI* magazine writer several years later. "I saw, my gosh, New York, ski trains, crowds. And I realized all you had to have is trails, tows, inns." Maybe things weren't as bad as he had thought.

He got considerable help for his ski-teaching efforts on February 7, 1937, when Stowe got its first mechanical means of uphill transportation. Driven by a 1927 Cadillac engine, a rope tow was installed on the newly cut practice slope near the Toll House, at the bottom of the Toll Road. With a tow and a place to teach, Ruschp discovered that he could do a pretty good

business in ski instruction. In his first season, he gave 1,100 lessons at $1 a lesson, and the tow, at 25 cents a ride, grossed $1,000. Ruschp made out better than expected, and despite a sweetened offer the next year from the folks out in Yellowstone, he decided to settle in for the long haul at Stowe. (It was a decision he wouldn't regret; by 1954, he was deemed, in an article in the *Saturday Evening Post*, to be "easily the most prosperous ski instructor in the world.")

Ruschp brought with him from Austria the rudiments of the so-called Arlberg technique, based on a teaching method developed in the 1930s by the famed ski-instruction pioneer Hannes Schneider. (Schneider would arrive in the United States three years after Ruschp, to open a ski school at Cranmore Mountain in New Hampshire.) Among other

Hi Folks.
The weather is cold,
The skiing fine,
Plan to be home
Sunday. Everyone
sends their regards,
Your loving
son
Dick

Mr. & Mrs. W. E. Woodruff
335 Blossom St
Fitchburg,
Mass.

*Above and right: The front and back of a
Stowe postcard showing a powder day
near the top of the Nose Dive, from 1949.
Opposite: The 200-car parking lot, cleared
in 1937 at the bottom of the Nose Dive,
was sometimes insufficient to accommodate
the crowds. The traffic jam along the
Mountain Road for the 1938 Eastern Ski
Championships was infamous.*

things, the Arlberg technique stressed keeping weight on the downhill ski and flexing the knees.

Ruschp's teaching skills were certainly in demand. People wanted to learn this hot new sport, and it wouldn't be long before they'd be looking for more of a challenge than the gentle slope at the Toll House. They would quickly want to test their newfound skills on the big mountain, and with skiers both climbing and descending trails at the same time in an era predating lifts, the potential for chaos was spectacular.

C. Minot "Minnie" Dole, a member of the New York Amateur Ski Club, described the crazed scene on the Nose Dive on a busy day in 1937. "Even the best of skiers did not necessarily have more than a passing knowledge of Arlberg turns," Dole wrote. "The cry of 'track!' meant something then. The downcoming

skier had to warn the upcoming skiers… When a climber heard that mournful call, he scrambled—putting at least one tree between him and the trail was a safe thing." Such circumstances inspired Dole to found the National Ski Patrol a year later, based on the country's first ski patrol developed a few years earlier by the Mt. Mansfield Ski Club (see page 61).

Skiing's popularity was spreading quickly throughout the country—by late 1938 the number of skiers in America would pass the one million mark—and no place in the country was more popular than Stowe. Perhaps the watershed event confirming Stowe's preeminence was the Eastern Ski Championships in 1937. The racing was originally scheduled to be held on the Thunderbolt Trail on Mt. Greylock in Massachusetts, but lack of snow forced the event to be moved to Stowe. The men of the

Mt. Mansfield Ski Club stepped in to offer the Nose Dive as a more-than-adequate substitute, figuring that hosting the race would be a prestigious feather in their cap. They had no idea what they were getting into.

A whopping 822 people bought train tickets to Waterbury to attend the event in Stowe. The incoming throng overwhelmed the local taxi service, consisting of two or three cars and a bus. Private motorists pitched in to help, and trucks had to be sent to Waterbury to carry all the skis to Stowe. Many more race fans came by car.

In a town in which accommodations totaled less than 300 beds for winter visitors, CCC cots had to be set up in the Memorial Building. "We filled all of the farms and village homes and even some of the barns with skiers," Craig Burt recalled.

On race day, the parking lot up at the mountain, able to hold about 200 cars, proved woefully inadequate. Depending on whose estimates you consider most credible, between 1,200 and 3,000 cars had to be parked along the Mountain Road, with up to 10,000 skiers and spectators in attendance. When the racing was done, the ensuing traffic jam didn't clear until after midnight.

The race weekend might not have come off as smoothly as its organizers had envisioned. It's probably not of great historical import that a Bavarian named Ulrich Beutter stole the show by winning the downhill on the Nose Dive. But as a moment in skiing history, the implications of the race weekend were clear. Skiing had taken root as a new national passion. And at the center of that new passion, Stowe had arrived. ▧

SUMMIT
MT. MANSFIELD
STOWE, VT.

In the era predating lifts on Mt. Mansfield, the hike to the summit could take as much as three hours, depending on snow conditions and a person's fitness level.

CHAPTER 3

A Starr Rises

Three runs a day. If you were in reasonably good shape and highly motivated, a three-run day on the Nose Dive would have been a pretty healthy dose of skiing in 1939. If you really pushed it, you might manage to squeeze in a fourth run. But to climb more than 2,000 vertical feet four times, while carrying your skis, was heavy grunting by any man's standards.

On the other hand, if you wanted to rack up dozens of runs in a day at the Toll House area, you could use the rope tow to yo-yo up and down the hill without taking much more than a deep breath. Mt. Mansfield skiers had to admit it: Downhill skiing without the hard work of uphill hiking was appealing, no doubt about it. But a rope tow up the innocent Toll House slope and a lift up mighty Mt. Mansfield were two different things altogether.

Building a chairlift to go up Mt. Mansfield would require no small amount of engineering ingenuity. You couldn't just go flipping through a catalog and order

*The rope tow (below) installed in the Toll House area in 1937 provided access only to a
short, easy slope. But for most Americans in the 1930s, with little or no skiing experience,
that was plenty. The demand for ski instruction (opposite) was considerable: Charging $1
a lesson, Sepp Ruschp and his team of Austrian instructors made a healthy income.*

yourself a lift; no company was producing chairlifts at the time. If
you wanted a lift, you would have to start from scratch. All of the
lift's components—the chairs, the towers, the cable—would have
to be custom designed and built.

Still, the idea wasn't entirely unprecedented. North America's
first chairlift was installed in 1936 on Dollar Mountain in Sun
Valley, Idaho, and a year later the first chairlift in the East was
installed at Belknap Mountain in Laconia, New Hampshire. In
addition, North America's first aerial tram opened at Cannon
Mountain in Franconia, New Hampshire, in 1938—a remarkable lift that would still be going strong more than 60 years later.

Stowe, which had established itself at the forefront of North
American skiing, was a logical place for a new lift, if for no other
reason than to remain positioned at the vanguard of skiing's

state of the art. The big question was: Who would foot the bill?
Building a chairlift more than a mile long up Mt. Mansfield
was an expensive proposition. The lifts in Sun Valley and
Laconia—much shorter and less ambitious—were small potatoes by comparison.

Reenter Roland Palmedo. Palmedo, with close ties to the
wealth of New York society to go with his abiding enthusiasm
for skiing, was well positioned to raise the lift-building funds. In
addition, as Ken Quackenbush (Palmedo's associate several
years later at Mad River Glen) put it: "He had a natural ability
to organize."

So in the fall of 1939, Palmedo set about organizing. Getting
a permit to put up a lift on state forest land was little more than a
formality; the man in charge of the permitting was Perry Merrill,

who'd already thrown his weight firmly behind the development of skiing on Mt. Mansfield. Palmedo then lined up a company, the American Steel and Wire Company, to manufacture the lift and its 86 single chairs.

Securing the financing was a job right up Palmedo's alley. As a Wall Street professional with well-honed financial acumen, he had a good feel for the kind of sales pitch that might lure some of the big players in New York on board. Strictly as a money-making proposition, running a ski lift had no track record. As such, it probably wasn't a wise investment, particularly given the considerable capital that would be required up front to build the thing. So Palmedo instead played up the romance of skiing. "Not all your money will be lost," he told potential investors, "and you'll be doing a wonderful thing for skiing."

The strategy—to de-emphasize the financial return and promote the skiing goodwill—apparently worked. In relatively short order, he managed to pull together a syndicate of partners willing and able to risk losing money for the sake of furthering the growing new sport. Among the syndicate's distinguished members were Godfrey Rockefeller of the Standard Oil Company and the legendary broadcaster Lowell Thomas. The syndicate pooled together $75,000 to form the Mt. Mansfield Lift Company, and in the late spring of 1940, with Charlie Lord overseeing the project, construction of the lift began.

Covering 6,330 feet, the chairlift would become the longest in the country and would rise 2,030 feet toward the Nose from the parking lot near Smugglers' Notch. When it was ready to go in November, however, the investors must have wondered at first

One of Stowe skiing's early advocates was the famed radio broadcaster, Lowell Thomas (second from left, above). Thomas often aired his weekly show from the Green Mountain Inn. The construction of the single chairlift on Mt. Mansfield in 1940 provided lift access to the trail network that Charlie Lord (right) created in the 1930s.

what they were getting themselves into. On November 17, before the lift opened to the public, the press was invited to preview this engineering marvel that would supposedly reinvent skiing. It was an inauspicious unveiling. The lift broke down in a blinding snowstorm, stranding 49 less-than-bedazzled members of the media for more than an hour before they could be evacuated.

The lift opened to the public three weeks later with the mechanical glitches apparently smoothed out. But the weather was again unaccommodating. A breakable crust had formed on the snow, caused by rain a few days earlier. The skiing, Lord declared without any attempt at positive-spin embellishment, was "poor."

Nevertheless, lift-served skiing was underway, and there could be no doubt that Stowe skiing would be forever changed. As Lord put it, "Skiing entered a new phase."

Lord was speaking in skiing terms, referring to the transition from a walk-up sport to a lift-served sport. But he might as well have been speaking in commercial terms, for the lift was the new centerpiece in a giant leap forward for Stowe skiing as a business enterprise rather than just a recreational pastime.

Skiing was no longer just the sport of a small group of enthusiasts; the lift made it something that could be enjoyed by the masses. The numbers in the first lift-served year indicated that Stowe was on the threshold of something big. During the walk-up era of the 1930s, an average winter day might see perhaps 15 hikers climb all the way up the mountain to ski. But in the winter of 1940-41, 57,266 passengers rode the new chairlift, at 60 cents a ride—an average of closer to 500 skiers a day.

Even if the skiing conditions throughout the winter of 1940-41 were classified by Lord as no better than "fairly good," gross receipts for the lift were $31,530. In the Toll House area, where the Austrian ski instructor Sepp Ruschp had set up shop, gross receipts from lodging, tow tickets and instruction were roughly $48,000.

Meanwhile, national and international acclaim for Stowe as a ski area continued to grow. In addition, the national media was jumping on the Stowe bandwagon, helping to spread the word. In 1940, *Look* magazine sent two photogenic University of Michigan students to Stowe for an article about the glories of a New England ski weekend. One of the students was Gerald Ford, who 34 years later would become President of the United States.

Not everyone in the Stowe area found this new state of affairs agreeable. A few loggers and outdoorspeople, who a decade earlier had pretty much had Mt. Mansfield to themselves in winter, expressed concerns that winter commercialization would ruin the mountain. But on the whole, the Stowe community was in concert with the sentiments of Craig Burt, himself a logger, who wrote: "It [skiing] is just as sure and as good-business as any summer development we have, and much better than some. And it comes at a time of year when finances and local morale are at a low point."

Local morale and finances, however, would have to wait a few years before being lifted. For as Stowe skiing appeared to be poised at the threshold of commercial success, World War II intervened. The bombing of Pearl Harbor on December 7, 1941, and America's immediate declaration of war reordered priorities in Stowe, as they did elsewhere across America.

Despite favorable snow conditions in the winter of 1942-43 ("an excellent winter—a long season with good skiing," according to Lord), the chairlift receipts had dropped to $23,086. Gas rationing limited the number of people able to visit Stowe by car, although fuel coupons were issued for the chairlift, which was considered to be a recreational necessity for off-duty servicemen.

Women were called upon to fill in as ski instructors, as able-bodied men were called away to war. Several members of the ski school and the ski patrol were recruited into the famed 10th Mountain Division, with its emphasis on ski-mountaineering skills; Sepp

Nose Dive Annie

Here is the way a legend is born: You are a beautiful young woman with a deep reservoir of energy and no small amount of inner toughness, living in what is largely the man's world of skiing in the 1930s. You prove your worthiness among your male peers by doing something few of them are willing or capable of doing— every winter day, regardless of weather, you hike up the Nose Dive and ski down it. The men take notice, to the point of anointing you with a nickname that will cement your legendary status: Nose Dive Annie.

This is the story of Anne Cooke, whose famous nickname alone has carried her into Stowe legend. Before the single chairlift was built in 1940, she was a fixture on the Nose Dive, becoming almost as well-known in the world of skiing as the trail itself. But her skiing exploits are only part of her story. She was also an accomplished pilot, one of just 25 women in the United States in the early 1940s to hold a commercial pilot's license. She proved to be a competent enough aviator to become an instructor for U.S. Army and Navy pilots—an occupation in which her nickname was presumably not so well received.

Ruschp, an experienced pilot, became a military flight trainer. Stowe skiing would amble through the war in a semidormant state, awaiting its next pulse of developmental energy.

While downhill skiing was shifting into gear in Stowe in the 1930s, Cornelius V. Starr was building an insurance empire based in Shanghai, China. When Charlie Lord and his crews first began cutting trails on Mt. Mansfield, Starr was underwriting trans-Pacific shipping operations and forging an insurance company that would grow to be one of the largest in the world.

In the mid 1930s, Starr was far removed from the world of skiing, and skiing was far from being foremost in Starr's mind. That the destiny of a ski area in Stowe would soon fall into the hands of a China-based insurance magnate was anything but foreseeable.

Stowe skiing and C.V. Starr were literally continents apart, both psychically and geographically.

Though described by those who knew him as a quiet and even shy man, Starr had an aptitude for entrepreneurship—an unusual knack for recognizing a business opportunity and capitalizing on it. Raised in a boardinghouse by his mother after his father died when he was two, the young Starr started his own business laundering uniforms for members of the Army's 24th Machine Gun Battalion in Fort Bragg, California, before World War I. Soon the business would be earning him $400 a month, a pretty healthy income for a guy still on the shy side of 25.

Starr would quickly outgrow the Fort Bragg operation, however. By the time he was 27 years old, he would find himself in

Shanghai—after a brief stint in Japan—setting up a business insuring cargo ships. He financed the fledgling enterprise with his own $10,000. Within a few years, that investment would flesh out into businesses worth millions in the Far East and 100 countries around the world.

By the late 1930s, however, Starr was facing the question that presumably must confront all men who have amassed a great fortune early in life: Where, beyond a business world in which he had already proven his mastery, was he to find new challenges? He had not been athletically inclined, so perhaps the challenge of the unfamiliar—the world of sport—is what drew Starr to skiing. Or perhaps he just needed a vacation and a change of scenery. For whatever reason, he decided in 1938 to take a trip to Sun Valley, Idaho, where the first chairlift in America had been erected two years earlier.

He was 47 years old at the time—not exactly an ideal age to enter a new sport—and he was hardly a natural athlete; he would never became more than a competent skier. But that initial ski trip lit an inextinguishable torch within Starr. As Peter Ruschp, Sepp's son, remembers when Starr would come to Stowe years later, "He was an enthusiast, absolutely passionate about the sport. He would ski everything and anything, in all conditions and all weather." One trip to Sun Valley, and Starr was hooked.

After Starr moved to New York in 1940, it was perhaps inevitable that his passion for skiing would draw him to Stowe. Here, after all, was a man willing to cross oceans and continents to satisfy his skiing habit; St. Anton, Austria, for example, would become a Starr favorite. In Stowe he had a world-class resort right in his own backyard, with America's longest chairlift, a

growing trail network, and one of the world's best ski schools, headed by Sepp Ruschp.

Starr first visited Stowe in the winter of 1943-44 to partake of the expertise of Ruschp, the master instructor. Initially it was all about skiing and learning to ski and nothing else. But it wasn't long before the skier's passion within Starr began to merge with his entrepreneurial instincts.

Impatience as much as anything started the business wheels turning. Disenchanted by standing in a long lift line with Ruschp one day in 1946, Starr wondered aloud if one chairlift, able to carry about 200 skiers an hour, had become inadequate in meeting the public's growing enthusiasm for skiing. Ruschp was listening.

So Starr and Ruschp began scheming. Ruschp had already

been contemplating the idea of building another lift on Mt. Mansfield; what he lacked was the money to pull it off. For Starr, of course, money was not a problem, but he didn't have Ruschp's local connections and expertise in the business of skiing. Together, however, they formed a formidable partnership.

Starr offered to put up half of the money to finance the building of a new T-bar on Mt. Mansfield. Ruschp, combining his own money with funds raised from local businesses, came up with the rest. By the winter of 1947, the T-bar, rising southeast of the chairlift, was up and running.

Still, looking at the larger picture, Starr observed that the ski area was evolving as anything but an efficient operation. Instead it was a jigsaw puzzle of companies. Palmedo and the New York syndicate controlled the Mt. Mansfield Lift Company, which

Gone But Not Forgotten

Eagan's Farm. Pinnacle Park Skiland. Marshall Hill. Underhill Ski Bowl. Scrolling through the history of Stowe-area skiing, you come across a handful of tiny ski areas that, like hundreds of others in New England and across America, have now faded into obsolescence. The New England Lost Ski Areas Project lists on its Web site more than 440 abandoned ski areas in New England, a list that is almost certainly incomplete.

After America's first rope tow went up in Woodstock, Vermont, in 1934, it seemed that almost every New England farmer with a small hill, a healthy piece of rope and a spare engine was getting into the ski business. On the western side of Mt. Mansfield, a 1,000-foot rope tow was strung up on Eagan's Farm in 1937. With the coming of World War II, however, the operation went out of business.

Another ski area on the western side of Mt. Mansfield, the Underhill Ski Bowl, managed to survive into the 1970s despite its diminutive stature; its vertical rise was just 245 feet. Not so successful was Pinnacle Park Skiland, a Waterbury area with a 1,000-foot rope tow and lights for night skiing, which began operation in 1939. The ski area ambitiously offered all-inclusive packages for ski-train visitors from the big cities, planned an annual winter carnival and ski ball, and even had Sepp Ruschp enlisted as a visiting instructor. Like Eagan's Farm, however, Pinnacle Park did not survive the war years.

Closer to home, a small ski area existed for a short period of time on Marshall Hill, near School Street in Stowe village. But perhaps the most curious of the now-defunct ski areas around Stowe was the man-made hill built in the mid 1960s at the Town and Country Motor Lodge on the Mountain Road.

At the time, the Town and Country was home to the only Playboy Club in Vermont, at a time when Playboy culture was at its zenith. Apparently flooded with cash due to the success of his business, the motel proprietor decided to literally create a ski area from scratch. Tons of dirt were trucked in and dumped on the motel lawn to form a "mountain" about 30 feet high. It was serviced by a 344-foot T-bar, but was not, apparently, a sufficient attraction to lure skiers away from Mt. Mansfield. By the early 1970s the mountain and lift were gone, and the lawn was back.

Left: The Lodge was one of five separate businesses that Starr and Ruschp consolidated into a single company in the 1950s. Opposite: Originally built by the C.C.C. in 1940 as a hut at the top of the single chair, the Octagon was subsequently expanded to accommodate expanding business.

owned the chairlift. Sepp Ruschp and other investors now owned the Mt. Mansfield Hotel Company, the principal asset of which was the Sepp Ruschp ski school. Starr and Ruschp headed up the Smugglers' Notch Lift Company, which owned the T-bar. The Burt Lumber Company owned most of the land not owned by the state. The Mt. Mansfield Ski Club was in charge of the ski patrol. Someone else owned the Lodge, the closest accommodations to the mountain.

Starr, with Ruschp as a partner, was beginning to envision in Stowe a major ski resort along the lines of what he had seen in Europe, in places like St. Anton. But to make that happen—or at least to jumpstart the process—he figured that all the pieces of the puzzle needed to be brought together as a single corporate entity.

And so he went about consolidating. He found a surprisingly willing seller in Palmedo's syndicate. The chairlift, after all, was beginning to become profitable, and a post-war boom in skiing promised to improve the business prospects. But Palmedo had from the start approached skiing in Stowe as a sportsman rather than an entrepreneur. As a principal in the New York Amateur Ski Club, he was an "amateur" skier in the true Latinate sense of the word—a person compelled by his love for sport. Stowe now appeared to be headed off on a more commercial tack.

"He was not a fan of commercialization," says Quackenbush, who would join forces with Palmedo at newly formed Mad River Glen a few years later. "It was one of the reasons he severed his relationship with Mt. Mansfield. There was a split in attitudes."

There was also a pretty good deal on the table. Starr in 1949 offered to buy the lift company for $300,000, four times what the syndicate had anted up in 1940. Palmedo might have decided to sell on principle, but in doing so, he also turned a handsome profit for the original investors. He would go on to establish Mad River Glen, 20 miles to the south, as what he perceived to be something of an anti-Stowe—a ski area that stressed the purity of skiing over commercial reward.

Starr no doubt shared Palmedo's appreciation for the purity of skiing. But he was at heart a businessman whose constitution wouldn't allow him to lose money, no matter how large or small the enterprise. He certainly hadn't made himself a success in business by throwing his money into projects that were hopelessly

unprofitable. "I always try to make money from my investments," was a Starr mantra.

So while the passions of a skier might have brought Starr to Stowe, the ingrained passion of a businessman dedicated to turning a profit is probably what made him stick around. He took unabashed pride in bringing a sound business sense into the operation of the growing ski area.

"When we came to Stowe," he told a *SKI* magazine writer several years later, "there were five companies, all fighting each other. Now they're all together, purring like kittens. And I believe we're the only big ski resort that makes money." In the winter of 1953-54, the Mt. Mansfield Company grossed more than $1 million for the first time. (Starr was well aware of the downside risk, however. In 1954, he told a friend: "I've never put more into Mt. Mansfield in one year than I can afford to lose.")

Even so, ski resorts have historically been built largely on dreams and not profit potential, and Starr was as much a dreamer as the next guy. After all, there were certainly places other than Stowe where Starr could have invested his money—government bonds, for instance—and gotten more bang for his buck. By the mid 1950s, his Mt. Mansfield Company was producing an annual gross profit of around six percent—a decent but by no means fortune-making return.

So the dream of building a world-class resort, not the reality of profitability, is what drove Starr to continue to pour money into Stowe. More trails were cut on Mt. Mansfield, and more lifts were installed. Starr brought fine art, fine wine, and a renowned European chef to the Lodge, the one hotel owned by the Mt. Mansfield Company, to bestow it with a kind of Old World style and panache.

He plied his global connections to bring renowned racers and instructors to Stowe, boosting the resort's reputation abroad. In one famously extravagant burst of inspiration, he paid to have the gold and silver medal winners in every Alpine skiing event in the 1952 Olympics flown to Stowe shortly after the Games ended in Oslo.

As M.J. Shaw, a long-time Stowe resident who would become executive director of the Mt. Mansfield Ski Club many years later, says: "He brought a lot of sophistication to the town that wasn't there before. The people who came to Stowe at that time were world travelers."

At the center of Starr's European vision was what he perceived to be the epitome of the Alpine experience—gliding down sun-drenched, wide-open slopes. He felt that if he could somehow pull that off in Stowe, he would have the St. Anton of Vermont.

Mt. Mansfield, however, was not where

Coats on a Rail

For much of the life of the single chair, the lift attendant would offer blankets to riders as they boarded the lift. On particularly cold or windy days, the blankets, which upon disembarking would be delivered to the summit attendant who could return them on descending chairs to the bottom, could be a welcome accompaniment.

Billy Kidd remembers the blankets as a kind of thermometer—a means of determining the coldness on any winter day. "You knew it was cold when you needed two blankets," says Kidd. "Even colder, and you needed three blankets. And only a few days every winter were four-blanket days."

Kidd, however, didn't need to worry too much about that. He was one of a number of Stowe regulars who brought to the mountain their own

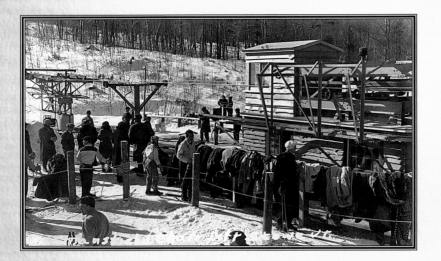

lift-riding apparel—in Kidd's case, a sheepskin coat, which, like the blankets, would ride an empty chair back to the bottom of lift, where it would await for the next ride up. Donning your own lift-riding outerwear was usually a little warmer and more water-repellent than using the standard blankets, which often became waterlogged or frozen when the weather turned particularly unpleasant.

But equally important, a personal coat was a sign of style and status. "You knew you were really cool at Stowe when you had your own coat to ride up with," says Kidd. The true haute couture of Stowe lift-riding was fur. Ed Rhodes, a Stowe historian, recalls that one New York woman in the early 1960s, after seeing all the personal coats slung over the rail in the lift-loading corral, remarked: "There must have been $400,000 worth of fur on that rail!"

Sepp Ruschp (center, holding phone), seen here overseeing a lift-construction project, was renowned as a hands-on manager.

it was going to happen. The state of Vermont, which owned most of the land on the mountain, had been generous in permitting Starr (and those who preceded him) to cut ski trails. The recreational and economic benefits that the growing ski area was bringing to the region were undeniable and, the government felt, in the state's interest. Still, cutting the kind of wide-open slopes Starr envisioned would undoubtedly have met stiff resistance.

Starr instead shifted his sights across the Smugglers' Notch road to Spruce Peak, a smaller mountain privately owned by the Burt Lumber Company. If he owned that land, Starr figured, he could proceed relatively unencumbered toward his vision of European perfection. In 1949 he made an offer to Burt that it couldn't refuse, and 3,500 acres on Spruce Peak came into the fold.

Like an artist set to begin a new painting, Starr now had in Spruce Peak a canvas to work with. Unfortunately, it was a canvas with a fundamental flaw. Spruce Peak faced south—great if you liked sun, but as any ski-trail designer could tell you, a southern exposure bodes poorly for snow quality. The wide trails Starr envisioned were cut, lifts were installed, and lodges were built. But all the capital at Starr's disposal couldn't resolve the fact that Spruce Peak's southern exposure, under the brunt of direct solar energy, didn't hold snow well.

Local historian Brian Lindner calls developments on Spruce Peak "grandiose plans that went down the drain." That might be an overly harsh assessment. Shaw's criticism is more to the point: "Spruce Peak [didn't] work well because you couldn't rely on the snow." In the 1950s, before the advent of snowmaking, the problem was particularly acute.

The Lodge under C.V. Starr's stewardship embraced both a casual, relaxed, atmosphere and an urbane elegance. It could boast in the 1950s a cordon-bleu chef, original art, and "the best wine cellar...to be found in any American inn, urban or rural," according to the Saturday Evening Post.

To be sure, on days when icy conditions prevailed on Mt. Mansfield, the softening effects of the sun on Spruce could make for much more enjoyable skiing. But more than likely, the southern exposure was a curse, ensuring at the very least a much shorter season than on Mt. Mansfield. In his summary of snow conditions for the winter of 1956-57, Charlie Lord wrote, "In general, a fairly good year on Mansfield but below average on Spruce." The theme would repeat itself from year to year: Snow conditions on Spruce were almost always several notches below conditions on Mt. Mansfield.

Nevertheless, Starr, along with Ruschp, persisted in the development on Spruce Peak through the 1950s. "It was the center of their focus through those years," says Sepp's son Peter. Big Spruce was a big deal back then."

But in truth, it was really only part of the much larger vision of creating in Stowe a world-class ski resort. That was a revolutionary idea at that time in North America. In the early 1950s, large full-service ski resorts in the United States were a rarity. Averell Harriman was developing a resort in Sun Valley and Walter Paepcke was trying to do the same in Aspen, Colorado. But major resort development in the United States wouldn't really hit its stride until the late 1950s and early 1960s, when places like Vail, Snowmass, Jackson Hole, Mammoth Mountain and Taos came into being.

Most ski areas up to that point were small family- or club-run operations. What Starr and Ruschp were doing in Stowe had little precedent in America. So a few miscalculations along the way—about the reliability of snow on Spruce Peak, for example —were probably unavoidable.

Building a resort in Stowe was more than just a combination of money and vision. It would be a matter of politics as well, and Starr from the start took care to play his political cards shrewdly. He recognized early the potential fallout that might be generated in provincial Vermont by a wealthy outsider coming in, tearing up the mountainsides and walking away with the profits. So from the start, and in virtually every developmental step he took, he carefully made sure to bring the local community into the equation. The point man in this effort was Sepp Ruschp, whose entrepreneurial drive proved a worthy match for Starr's.

When it came to financing projects—the Mt. Mansfield T-bar, the Spruce Peak development and so on—Starr would typically put up only about half the money. Ruschp would then be turned loose on the local community to raise the balance. He proved to be remarkably adept at it by courting individuals, small businesses and banks. "He was good at talking to the business world, expressing his enthusiasm for skiing and selling the sport," says son Peter. Ruschp seemed to have little problem raising money, but equally important, a broad sector of the Stowe community was brought into the fold, with a vested interest in the success of the growing resort.

Starr considered one of his strengths as a businessman to be his ability to put good management in place, or, as Peter Ruschp says, "his ability to get the right people in the right place at the right time." In Sepp Ruschp, Starr had found the ideal man for the job and time. Not only was Ruschp an effective money-raiser, he also proved to be an able, hands-on manager full of energy and commitment. He, after all, had ideas for a more substantial resort at Stowe before Starr arrived, even going so far as to draw up blueprints. He simply had lacked the seed money that Starr provided.

For Starr, whose fortune had been forged in other fields of endeavor, building a ski area at Stowe was essentially an avocation. (Starr himself conceded that owning a ski resort was really little more than a bauble, a status symbol for people of great wealth. "There is no difference," he said, "in having a yacht, or a racing stable, or an actress, or a ski resort.") For Ruschp, however, this was his life's business, and he threw himself into the minutiae of the day-to-day operations of the company.

"He ran a tight ship," says Shaw, meaning he brought to his position as president of the Mt. Mansfield Company a Teutonic sense of regimentation and single-mindedness. But he still managed to build an effective and even warm relationship with most of the people he worked with. He made a point of personally getting to know virtually everyone who worked for the company. "It was very much a family affair back then," says Peter Ruschp, for whom that was literally the case.

When problems arose, Sepp was a hands-on manager. Peter Ruschp remembers a time when the chairlift broke down on New Year's Eve and Sepp was right there with the work crews, hands deep in grease repairing the gear box. Some workers might have groused at the intrusion— a case of management sticking its nose in where it didn't belong. But Ruschp sidestepped that potential problem by ordering a case of champagne, which he shared with the crew in celebration when the repair work was finished. "He was an expediter," says Peter. "If there was a problem, he'd steamroll over it."

"Stowe [in the 1950s and 1960s] pretty much epitomized New England skiing,"

The Moriarty Hat

She was, in a manner of speaking, the mother of all hats, which may be why she was widely known as Ma. In 1956, Anabel "Ma" Moriarty knitted a wool cap for her son, Marvin, a member of the U.S. Olympic Ski Team that year. Marvin was rushing off to the Olympics, and Anabel, without enough time to finish the hat properly, stitched together the top in a hurry, resulting in a peaked, triangular shape. The rest is hat history.

The hastily completed hat, having debuted on the head of a handsome young Olympian, quickly became a central element of skiing's fashion iconography from the late 1950s on. Anabel began mass production of the hat shortly after Marvin returned from the Olympics, knitting hats herself in the Moriarty home.

The business flourished so rapidly that by the mid 1960s, Anabel had a team of 14 knitters producing about 1,000 hats a week.

The hat—in various forms, imitations and incarnations—has remained a staple of skiing fashion since. When Billy Kidd, Stowe's most famous Olympian, won a silver medal in the 1964 slalom, he did so wearing a Moriarty hat. At the height of the hat's popularity in the 1970s, it was virtually the only hat design that any serious and self-respecting skier would be seen in— especially any serious and self-respecting skier from Stowe.

In fact, arguably no single fashion statement in skiing in the past 50 years has been so recognizable and enduring as the Moriarty hat. And the legacy marches on; the Moriarty Hat and Sweater Shop continues to do a thriving business in Stowe.

says Quackenbush. "Mt. Mansfield was the biggest and most Alpine mountain. It was the center of social focus for people who considered themselves real skiers."

But by the late 1960s, Stowe's high tide had begun to ebb. In 1968, the 7,000-foot-long gondola lift, terminating at the elegant Cliff House below the Chin and providing access to five newly cut trails, opened for business. It should have heralded the dawning of a new era in Stowe history, bringing to the resort the sort of sunny, open-slope skiing that never really materialized on Spruce Peak. But the excitement surrounding the gondola's opening was dampened by two events that December that may have been portents for the coming years.

On December 20, C.V. Starr died at age 77, ending two decades of dedicated stewardship. And on New Year's Eve, one of the brand-new gondola cars fell from the cable, injuring four people, one seriously. The accident made the kind of national news previously unfamiliar in Stowe circles; when the resort had made headlines in the past, the news was usually about some inspiring new development on the mountain, or the visitation of some foreign dignitary. This had always been a magical place where things just weren't supposed to go wrong.

What really slowed Stowe's momentum from the late 1960s on, however, was the rise of competition. A whole host of new resorts had sprung up in the West—Vail, Snowmass, Jackson Hole, Snowbird and others. Closer to home, Killington was making waves with brash, youthful promotion and a new reliance on snowmaking. Sugarbush was trying to steal some of Stowe's international cache by hiring the famously debonair ski instructor Stein Eriksen.

Stowe moved into this newly competitive environment with some reluctance. In the 1980s, a *Travel & Leisure* reporter wrote: "The Mountain Company, as locals call the ski area, and indeed much of the town of Stowe, arrogantly looked down on the upstarts and chose to do nothing but wear its reputation until it was threadbare."

In particular, Stowe dragged its feet in installing snowmaking while many of its competitors moved forward aggressively. Limited snowmaking was installed on Spruce Peak in 1967, but Ruschp, as his son Peter says, "was not happy about it. If Killington was getting into snowmaking, everyone was going to have to do it. And it was just going to be too expensive." It wasn't until the winter of 1979-80 that the first snowmaking was installed on Mt. Mansfield. By then, Killington had hundreds of acres covered, not only ensuring a longer season but also ensuring snow coverage for the critical Christmas–New Year's Day period.

When Starr passed on, a leadership vacuum was inevitable. "C.V. and Sepp had a very paternal attitude" toward running the resort, says Shaw. This was their baby, their offspring that they had together reared into the adulthood of international acclaim. With Starr's passing, Stowe lost its visionary. The resort was no longer Starr's baby but a small part of the American International Group (AIG), the multibillion-dollar company that Starr left behind. When AIG bought out Ruschp and other minor investors to secure full ownership of the resort, the connections between the resort and its roots were further loosened.

*The original gondola, (left) installed in 1968, was 7,000
feet long and provided access to five new trails beneath
the Chin. Modern snowmaking and slope grooming
(below) have vastly improved the snow surface.*

Through the next couple of decades, the resort more or less maintained the status quo while the competition marched forward. Some local critics claimed that AIG had lost interest in the resort and wasn't putting enough money into it. In fact, significant investments were made. A high-speed quad was installed to replace the single and double chairs that ran side by side on Mt. Mansfield. A new gondola replaced the original gondola, with expanded new base facilities. Snowmaking was expanded (though not always with great success; many Stowe locals recall the glacial mound of ice that formed one year at the top of the National trail, the result of one particularly inept snowmaking effort). But there was no headlining expansion of terrain, no spectacular new lifts or lodges built, no groundbreaking statement to reaffirm

Stowe's status at the higher ground of American skiing.

Still, it would hardly be accurate to suggest that Stowe went into a tailspin from the late 1960s on. The resort simply stood its ground while its competitors played catch-up, and there was plenty of room for that. After all, Stowe as a ski area had at least a 20-year head start on the competition.

And even if Stowe lost some of its éclat as a resort of international acclaim, it still held on to something it could never lose. What inspired Palmedo in the 1930s and Starr in the decades to follow would remain unshakably intact: the quality of the skiing. Mt. Mansfield was still the biggest, most Alpine mountain in the neighborhood. And Stowe was still the self-proclaimed Ski Capital of the East, with skiing terrain unsurpassed in the Northeast. ▨

In the winter of 2000-01, when
388 inches fell on Mt. Mansfield, lines
that were rarely even skiable were skied.

C H A P T E R **4**

Ski Capital of the East

After a winter as profoundly snowy as the winter of 2000-01, memories become immortal. Everyone living in Stowe that winter seems to have some indestructibly vivid recollection of snow of diluvian proportions—of buried houses, unplowable driveways, sagging roofs and, on Mt. Mansfield, powder days stacked one atop the other in a winter-long, snowy blur.

Extreme skiers and snowboarders were taking on lines—the northwest face of the Nose, cliff areas between the Nose and the Chin, rock-slide chutes on the eastern faces of Smugglers' Notch—that in some cases had probably never before been skied. The snow filled in every crack and crevice in the mountain facade to the point where even the unskiable—sheer cliffs above the Cliff House, for example—became skiable, at least for the handful of locals talented and perhaps crazy enough to pull it off. But the snow piled up on open trails, too, and even when the powder was all tracked up and packed out, the mogul skiing on a classic mogul

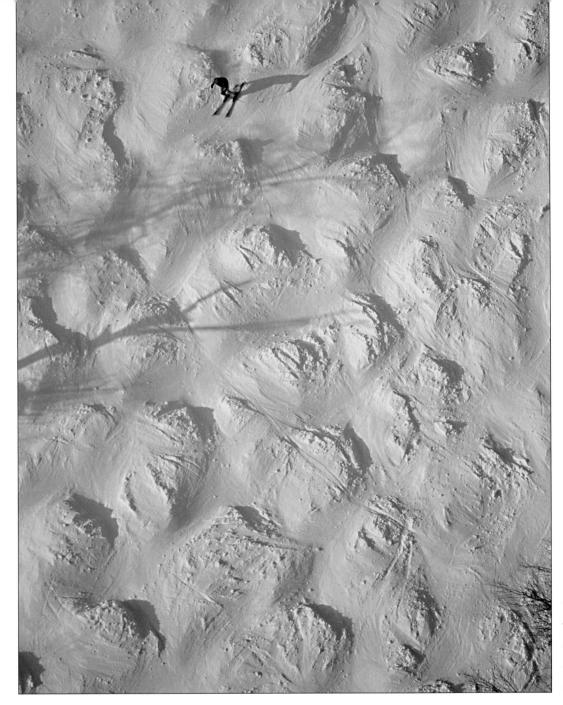

Because of the high caliber of skier at Stowe, the moguls that form on trails like National are usually well-rounded and symmetrical.

trail like National or Starr was as good as mogul skiing gets anywhere in the world. Skiers and snowboarders in Stowe will never allow themselves to forget such things.

When winter finally gave up in the middle of April, opening the way for something resembling spring, the official snowfall total for Mt. Mansfield was 388 inches. But that number seems, by common agreement among knowledgeable skiers in Stowe, to represent an underaccounting. High on the mountain, the snowfall appeared to have been considerably greater than 388 inches.

After all, a two-foot extension had to be attached to the top of the snow stake below the Nose on Mt. Mansfield, where WCAX-TV keeps a semi-official record of the settled snowpack on the mountain. The original stake, 12 feet tall, would have been completely buried when the last heavy wave of snow came through toward the end of March. In the nearly 50 years of the stake's existence, it had never accumulated like that. When you're talking about a settled snowpack of 12 feet or more, there's a pretty good chance you're talking about a snowfall total exceeding 400 inches.

Not every winter, past or future, can resemble the winter of 2000-01. Taking nothing other than the quality of snow into account, Stowe skiing and snowboarding in the winter of 2000-01 was Stowe at its best. But snow, however plentiful it might be in any given winter, is almost literally icing on a cake of complex composition that extends beyond skiing itself and into the culture of skiing life at Stowe.

Through the 1960s, Stowe's glamorous reputation attracted many celebrities, including Ted Kennedy (top left); Jackie Kennedy (left, with white hat) with her children John (to Jackie's left) and Caroline (seated); and the Dalai Lama (above).

Leaving aside for the moment the terrain that has made Stowe famous, consider Stowe skiing in strictly demographic terms. Through more than two decades of post-war resort building, Sepp Ruschp and C.V. Starr, Stowe's two developmental masterminds, envisioned a ski destination of international reputation and glamour. That vision probably reached its zenith somewhere in the 1950s and 1960s, when Stowe was hosting such events as the American International races and when visits by celebrities from the Dalai Lama to the Kennedy family gave Stowe a certain voguish panache.

Stowe's glamorous reputation might have sputtered through the 1970s and 1980s, due in part to the passing first of Starr and then Ruschp. Also, such famous Western resorts as Vail and Aspen were on the rise. But by the turn of the millennium, Stowe (the ski area), under the guidance of AIG, the insurance conglomerate that Starr left behind, seemed to have regained its equilibrium, reestablishing itself on the global map of important ski destinations.

There are numbers to verify it. According to statistics from the National Ski Areas Association, in the five years between 1997 and 2002, international visitors (Canadians not included) represented eight percent of Stowe's market. That's a substantial international representation in New England, where ski resorts see almost all of their visitors coming from nearby Northeastern states. In fact, in that five-year period, skiers from England ranked sixth in number among Stowe visitors, behind visitors from Vermont, Massachusetts, New York, Connecticut and New Jersey.

The University of Vermont Catamounts ski team, a perennial
favorite for NCAA title, regularly trains at Stowe.

A casual aural survey, on an average day in the base lodge, can produce a language stew that affirms the statistics: British accents mixing with French, Swedish and who knows what else. It lends to the experience of skiing at Stowe an internationally tinged aura rarely encountered elsewhere in the Northeast.

But there is another aura, more endemic and enduring, that permeates the Stowe ski scene: Stowe brings together the core of Eastern skiing's hardcore. The number of highly talented skiers and snowboarders per capita is arguably higher in Stowe than anywhere else in the Northeast and is a reasonable match for anywhere else in the country.

That can be attributed in part to the ski-industry congregation that has set up shop in nearby Burlington. The headquarters of several major ski and snowboard companies are based in Burlington, including Rossignol, Dynastar, Burton and Lange. On any given day at Stowe, the lift lines are well populated with company representatives attired in uniforms with conspicuous company logos and equipped with gear so up-to-date that much of it has yet to reach ski stores and the general public. In fact, many of the ski and snowboard companies use Stowe as a testing ground for new products still in development. As Charlie Adams, a Dynastar executive, notes, "It's so efficient. With the high-speed quad and so much vertical, you can get an amazing amount of testing done in just two hours." Whether testing or just free skiing, the company reps, most of them ex-racers, ski hard, fast and well.

The ski-industry cavalcade is joined on the mountain by members of the University of Vermont ski team, an annual

The Stone Hut

It was originally conceived and built by the Civilian Conservation Corps (CCC) in 1935-36 as a mountain-top warming hut. It survives today, intact and modestly refurbished, to provide rudimentary accommodations for skiers and snowboarders in winter and hikers in summer. For anyone willing to sleep in tight quarters on a wood platform with heat furnished by a wood-burning stove, Vermont Youth Hostels is ready to take reservations. For backcountry skiers, the Stone Hut beneath the Nose is a perfectly comfortable place to spend a winter night.

But the story of the Stone Hut has a counter-cultural edge to it, too, for the hut over the years has served as a skier's (and snowboarder's) version of an after-hours club of sorts. That's a tradition that dates back to the Stone Hut Gang, a group of young and sometimes reckless skiers in the 1940s who, as one Stone Hutter wrote, "really took over the mountain" when "the lift had stopped, the thundering herd had gone down and the patrol had rounded up the last straggler."

The Stone Hut Gang liked to ski in the last vestiges of sunlight, climbing back up to the hut in the dark for a steak-and-beer dinner to be ready for more skiing first thing in the morning, before the lifts opened. Sometimes they wouldn't wait that long, perhaps depending on how much beer had been consumed. As Stone Hutter Huntley Palmer wrote in 1944, "Even darkness didn't stop them, and who but a Stone Hutter would be crazy (and energetic) enough to run the Toll Road after dark at 10 below just to take in the movies at Stowe, and then climb back after midnight?"

The gang was also renowned for organizing the Merry Go Round races in the 1940s, in which competitors had to run downhill races on four trails in the same day: the Nose Dive, Chin Clip, the Bruce and Steeple (see Chapter 6). For a time, the Stone Hut Gang was a relatively well-organized operation, with its own "official publication," entitled *Elevation 3550.*

Skiers and snowboarders have carried on the after-hours tradition of the Stone Hut Gang through the years, in spirit if not in name. In fact, the Stone Hut tradition was a boon for the first generation of snowboarders, before snowboarding was permitted on most resort trails in 1987. Prior to that, the only way to ride on the resort trails was to hike to the Stone Hut for riding after and before the lifts were open.

Whether snowboarding or skiing, past or present, the Stone Hut experience has always been as much about backcountry bonding as it has the skiing itself. As Robert Fletcher, the so-called "scribe of the Stone Hut Gang," wrote in an edition of *Elevation 3550,* how many skiers could claim, after a sunset run on the mountain, that they had "polished off…steaks with a can of Pabst's sweetest nectar as a diluent, while the wind howled outside and the temperature dropped 10 degrees an hour? Brother, that's skiing—Stone Hut style."

contender for the title of national collegiate champion.
When team members aren't race training, they are often
seen blitzing down the mountain in race suits of green and
yellow Lycra, sometimes achieving speeds high enough to
intimidate the skiing public and cause perturbation among
the ski patrol.

Throw into that high-caliber mix the visible presence of a
ski school that has been rated among the top 10 in the country
by *SKI* magazine. It is manned by a corps of top-flight instructors from such locales as Europe, South America and
Australia, as well as the United States. Stu Campbell, who for
10 years was the ski school's technical director, explains why
they come to Stowe: "You have ski instructors with credentials
a mile long who keep gravitating back, because they love it—

they love being on this mountain." They are drawn in particular to the challenges of the mountain, which, says Campbell,
are capable of making some of the best instructors in the world
even better.

But ultimately, the culture of Stowe skiing is primarily about
the local folk—all the skiers and snowboarders raised on the
inherent and complex challenges that the mountain presents,
bred on high-caliber racing through the Mt. Mansfield Ski
Club, and driven by a passion for their mountain that is unparal-
leled in Eastern skiing. So passionate are local skiers that they
have a habit of speaking of their home turf rhapsodically. Says
Adams, who has lived in Stowe for more than 15 years: "The
place has such spirit. It's so hardcore. It's just amazing how soul-
ful Stowe really is."

Left: In the era before modern grooming, competitors and volunteers had to pack trails like the Nose Dive with their skis to prepare for racing. Above: Charlie Lord and Dorothy Warner sartorially showing off Stowe's Tyrolian connection.

Still, for all the personality and passion that characterizes Stowe skiing, it is the mountain itself that makes the ski area what it is. You can build all the facilities, offer all the amenities, assemble all the great skiers you can find, and do all the clever marketing you want. But without a first-rate mountain and a decent amount of snow to cover it, you won't go far as a ski area. As Billy Kidd says of Stowe, "The whole reason it became an interesting and credible ski resort was because there was a real mountain."

Actually, it's more complicated than that, for the ski area comprises not one but two mountains—Mansfield and Spruce—and Mansfield alone is massive enough to seem sometimes like two or more mountains fused together. As a result, the ski area over the years has been pieced together as a giant, mutating jigsaw

puzzle, spreading over time from Mt. Mansfield to Spruce Peak, across the road leading through Smugglers' Notch, and back. Terrain-wise, there are four basic pieces to the puzzle: the mostly gentle terrain of Spruce Peak; the easy-going, intermediate terrain serviced by the gondola below the Chin; the more challenging terrain beneath the Nose; and all the terrain that exists beyond the designated trail network.

Of course it took years of trail cutting, lift building and terrain shaping to bring Stowe to this point. But it all began with the efforts and vision of Charlie Lord. Those who love Stowe lay praise at Lord's feet with an almost apostolic veneration, hailing his genius in conceptualizing the initial trail network developed from the 1930s through the 1960s. "The runs run downhill as naturally as water," says Stu Campbell. "Charlie had an engi-

neer's understanding of fall line and sun angle and wind direction and terrain. All of us at Stowe owe a huge debt of gratitude to Charlie."

The Nose Dive was Lord's initial masterpiece, the trail that made Stowe famous. The Nose Dive, cut in 1934, wasn't the first trail cut on Mt. Mansfield, a distinction that goes to the Bruce, now a backcountry trail. But the Nose Dive was the first trail to be served by the first lift, the single chair installed in 1940. It was the trail used for the first sanctioned racing in Stowe, and the first trail to scare the daylights out of skiers trying to negotiate its infamous (and infamously icy) seven turns at the top.

The Nose Dive today is not what it once was; the beast has been tamed. The seven turns are no more, although a nasty hairpin at the top of today's Nose Dive gives at least some intimation

of what the trail was like in the days when famous racers from Dick Durrance to Stein Eriksen to Billy Kidd had to deal with its treacheries. Otherwise, the Nose Dive has mellowed with age, a trail that now is for the most part a wide, groomed avenue that has become a favorite among advanced-intermediate cruisers.

So the fear factor has been passed on to the neighboring Front Four—National, Lift Line, Goat and Starr, four trails that spill down from the Nose like four white braids. They are relative youths alongside the Nose Dive. The eldest of the Front Four is National, cut in conjunction with the Stowe's hosting of the National Championships in 1952. Sepp Ruschp called it "a real championship slalom course." That wasn't just because the trail had "the ideal northeast exposure [to] hold snow until late in spring." National was also steep, according to Ruschp's calcula-

The fabulous Front Four, Goat (the narrow trail left of the Nose),
Liftline, National (crossing liftline) and Starr. They are Eastern skiing at its most
challenging—particularly when Lookout (left of Starr) is added to the package.

tions, dropping more than 1,000 vertical feet in less than half a mile. That represented a consistent steepness that the Nose Dive couldn't match.

But when the Goat and Starr were cut in 1960, even National began to look almost tame. At least National was wide, between 100 and 150 feet across when first cut. That width provided a margin for error unavailable on the narrower and steeper Goat and Starr. With Lift Line tossed into the mix, this was a concentrated package of expert terrain that no other ski area in the East could match.

The ascendancy of the four famous trails into the pantheon of North American greatness was swift. By the mid 1960s, the Front Four had earned a national reputation for sheer intimidation that might have surpassed the precedent set by the Nose

Dive. After all, there were four trails, not just one, to scare you silly. Although widening and grading of National and Lift Line over the years made the trails somewhat easier to negotiate, the reputation for intimidation remains intact and deserved.

The Front Four present a daunting challenge not simply because of their steepness. By a broadly applied standard—putting the Front Four alongside steep runs of the Rockies or the Alps—the Front Four can be considered only moderately steep. The steeper sections of Starr and Goat—the steepest pitches on Mt. Mansfield's entire trail network— register in at over 70 percent. That's plenty steep. But when compared with, say, a couloir in Chamonix, France, where a fall can be fatal, it comes across as positively mellow.

Instead, the challenge of the Front Four is "technical," a term

Thanks to widening and grooming, the top of the Nose Dive now is not as frightening as it was in the 1940s and 1950s, when it was one of the top downhill courses in America.

expert skiers apply to an amalgam of factors—narrowness, variations in pitch and terrain, the presence of rocks, ice and other obstacles—of which steepness is just one considered element. No trail at Stowe epitomizes that technical challenge more overtly than the Goat.

The Goat is steep. The Goat is narrow. The Goat features a double fall line, in which the trail slants harshly downward from right to left. The Goat is full of what ski-area proprietors euphemistically call "unmarked obstacles" and mountaineering types sometimes call "objective hazards"—rocks, stumps, patches of solid ice and other niceties to avoid. And because of the gravitational pull of the double fall line, the trees on the left side of the trail are always in play. A fall on the Goat is almost certain to exact painful consequences.

On the face of it, this would not seem to be the recipe for pleasurable skiing. Yet experienced Stowe skiers speak of the Goat as they might speak of a partner in a long-running love affair. Steve Jones, an instructor, shop manager and basic ski bum in Stowe since the 1970s, says of the Goat, "It is one of the most challenging runs in the U.S. because of its terrain and contours. To have something like that here in the East—in Stowe—is amazing."

What satisfies skiers like Jones is that the Goat rewards technical proficiency, the skill not only to turn precisely but also to turn according to the demands of the trail, not according to the skier's whim. The pleasure borders on latent masochism, for as Jones says, with great enthusiasm, "If you make one little error on the Goat, you are punished."

Hank Lunde, president of Stowe Mountain Resort, sprinkles the word "community" liberally throughout his discussion of the resort's master plan, like an artist dabbing prominent flecks of paint on a canvas. "This is a community plan," Lunde says of a projected 10-year program to upgrade the resort. "The future of Stowe [the resort] is the future of the community at large."

There is good reason to be so judicious in acknowledging the inclusion of the entire Stowe community in the plan. As *Stowe Reporter* publisher Biddle Duke says, "The relationship between the mountain and the community is so strong that it's hard to explain where it begins and ends." Or as Lunde says, "This is their mountain," referring primarily to the people of Stowe. "We're re-energizing the historic patterns of use." That is why the resort brought representatives from 27 separate groups, speaking for various community and regional commercial interests, into the dialogue in developing the plan.

Hank Lunde

The seeds of the plan were first sowed in 1997, when the resort faced a need to upgrade its system of withdrawing water from local streams for snowmaking. A decision was made that, if an expensive and comprehensive snowmaking overhaul was in order, perhaps it was time to forge a more comprehensive plan for the resort's future.

The result, after several years of discussion and modification, is a plan that, according to Lunde, represents not only relatively modest development of on- and off-mountain facilities but also the end of the line in resort expansion. "This is it," he says. "There won't be a Phase II or Phase III."

Most of the development is focused on Spruce Peak, where the resort will build a "hamlet," comprising a hotel, a condominium hotel, a new base lodge and retail space. The skiing at Spruce Peak will also undergo a serious overhaul. While the terrain under the gondola helped bring legitimate intermediate skiing to Stowe in 1968, Lunde believes that it is still too challenging for many lower-level intermediates. "The image of the ski area is still an upper-level image," says Lunde.

The developments at Spruce Peak are aimed at softening that image, particularly in improving terrain for beginning and novice skiers. New, faster lifts, snowmaking all the way to the top of Big Spruce and trail improvements are all elements of the master plan.

Not all of the Stowe community is comfortable with the developments. "A good number of the voters don't want to see [the resort] expanded," says M.J. Shaw, a Stowe-area resident and former executive director of the Mt. Mansfield Ski Club. "I'm not sure the town can handle it."

Concerns have been expressed about everything from an increase in traffic on the Mountain Road to a possible loss of town business to the new lodging and retail enterprises on the mountain.

But Lunde insists that the master plan has been developed not only with a sensitivity toward the community's needs but with the participation of the community. "We really need the town," he says. "If we don't have a vibrant town, we go backward. There has been a very strong understanding here that neither one—the town or the resort—is as strong alone as we are together."

Left: Late afternoon on the Nose Dive, with a storm coming through Smugglers Notch in the background. Opposite: A clear cold morning at the Octagon and the Forerunner quad chair. Note the wind ripples in the snow.

For a short while, National inflicted its own, unique brand of punishment. Snowmaking was first installed at Stowe in 1967, on Spruce Peak. But snowmaking didn't arrive on Mt. Mansfield until 1980, and the initial efforts to make snow on the top of National produced less than satisfying results.

Local skiers remember what in effect was a glacial tongue of man-made ice at the top of the trail. Because of the angle at which the snow guns delivered their discharge to the slope, the ice formed a kind of whaleback rollover that on the downhill side effectively made the top of National even steeper than it already was. The surface was so hard and steep that new snow, failing to bond with the ice, would sometimes literally avalanche down the trail.

This obviously was not the sort of skiing terrain to appeal to the general public, but some members of the ski school regarded the icefall at the top of National as a consummate challenge. They dubbed the icy monstrosity Larry's Lump in honor of Larry Asam, one of their brethren. Their idea of fun was to try to ski on the ice by jumping in the air and jamming their edges into the surface, to see if somehow they could magically stick. It was a true test of strength, timing and precision.

And it wasn't easy, although some of the instructors thought they were pretty good at it—at least until Phil Mahre, the great American racer, showed up one day. The instructors challenged him to try their pet exercise, figuring that something of such difficulty was probably capable of humbling even the best ski racer in the world.

Instead, Mahre reciprocated by delivering to the instructors his own lesson in humility. "He jumped up in the air," Steve Jones

recalls, "and he absolutely chiseled ice off when his edges hit. He was so strong and so precise. Phil blew the doors off all of us."

In some cases the challenge of the Front Four comes not only from the terrain itself but from a pressure to perform—to be at your flawless best—in the presence of so many of the country's best skiers. Stu Campbell considers Lift Line his favorite trail on the mountain precisely because of the knowledgeable, talented and critical audience passing by overhead. "Lift Line is directly in the fall line, and it has a [steep] pitch that forces you to make a good turn, every turn," says Campbell. "The steepness isn't excessive, but it is always demanding, and with people above you scrutinizing everything you do, it forces you to ski better."

"The Front Four are the bar," says local skier Jay Bowen. "They are the real test in the East of whether you're an expert."

And they might fairly be considered the Front Five, for alongside Starr runs Lookout, as much of an expert's test as any of the other four. And because it hasn't been unofficially enshrined in the Front Four pantheon, it is often overlooked, which is why Charlie Adams calls Lookout his favorite trail on the mountain. "It doesn't get a lot of traffic, like the Front Four," says Adams. "Because of that, on a powder day, it keeps snow longer." So whether it is the Front Five or Front Four, it all comes together in what is arguably the most challenging cluster of expert trails in the East.

Just how much the Front Four—both in reputation and reality—discouraged nonexperts from coming to Stowe is anybody's guess. Through most of the 1960s, Stowe was widely regarded as

pretty much an experts-only area. The image, while not entirely accurate, was also not entirely unjustified. But when the first gondola (the precursor to the current gondola) was erected in 1968, the experts-only image was laid to rest.

Up until that point, Stowe lacked long, wide, moderately pitched runs, set straight down the fall line, with a smooth and even surface for easy grooming. Such runs, characteristic of a more modern trail-cutting philosophy, were becoming popular at resorts in the West, at places like Vail and Snowmass. They were becoming the bread and butter of resorts trying to attract the vacationing, recreational skier—someone looking less for challenge than for a relaxing, easy-going day on the mountain.

Most of the terrain under the Nose—including not just the Front Four but other, less formidable trails—presented more of a challenge than the occasional, recreational skier wanted to deal with. It was less than ideal for families with small kids. Because much of the original trail-clearing work was done by hand, the trail cutters' route of choice was often the path of least resistance. As a trail cutter in the early days, you had to work with the contours of the mountain; you couldn't just dynamite them into smooth, straight-line submission. And Charlie Lord's concept of trail design played heavily on a spirit of intrigue and challenge, not just dead-on-the-fall-line simplicity.

The result in Lord, for example—the trail that bears Charlie's name—was a trail of constantly varying pitch and fall line, following the natural contours of the mountain in tracing a semicircular course down the mountain. It was a trail on

which you needed to be alert at all times for subtle changes in pitch or direction. When first cut, it was just 20 to 50 feet wide.

Lord has, over the years been widened, and some of its quirky contours have been smoothed out. But it can still be an enigma to intermediates looking for the type of straightforward, uncomplicated run they might find at a place like Vail or Snowmass. After all, Lord, in effect, represents an effort to create an intermediate run on a part of the mountain that is fundamentally too steep for intermediate skiing. If you want straight-on-the-fall-line skiing under the Nose, you end up with Starr or National.

So if intermediate terrain under the Nose was hard to come by, where else might it be found? C.V. Starr and Sepp Ruschp came upon at least a partial solution with the erection of a T-bar on Mt. Mansfield in 1946. The T-bar, to the left of the single chair on the mountain's southeastern flank, served a new network of trails that, while shorter than the trails from the chairlift, were also, on the whole, less steep. (That terrain is now served by a triple chair, installed in 1985.)

If the T-bar had a shortcoming, however, it was that the runs were relatively short. The vertical rise wasn't much more than 1,000 feet. So Starr and Ruschp soon turned their eyes to Spruce Peak, more robust with its 1,600 vertical feet. On the southern face of Spruce, the pitch averaged between nine and 28 percent and never exceeded 45 percent, good stuff for beginners and intermediates. Spruce Peak was south-facing and sunny, offering a comfortable balm for less-than hardcore skiers. But that southern exposure also proved to be a curse, particular in the 1950s and 1960s, before the extensive use of snowmaking. The snow

conditions, under the melting influence of the sun, weren't always reliably good.

So the two visionaries looked elsewhere again, returning their sights to Mt. Mansfield. For intermediate skiing, the flanks of the mountain under the Chin seemed ideal. The terrain lay at a consistently intermediate pitch—averaging about 25 percent and never exceeding 45 percent—for more than 2,000 vertical feet. The terrain under the Chin was, by and large, sun-drenched terrain, thanks to a more easterly exposure than that of the predominately north-facing trail network beneath the Nose. Still, it wasn't directly south-facing like the trails on Spruce Peak, sparing it the snow-wrecking onslaught of direct solar radiation.

With the rocky bulwark of the Chin rising 650 feet above the gondola terminal, there was at least some protection from bitter, cold winds out of the northwest. The enclosed gondola itself offered additional protection from the elements. And the Cliff House, housing the gondola's summit terminal, was the kind of warm, high-mountain way station more commonly found at Alpine resorts than in New England.

A structure large enough to house a substantial restaurant, the Cliff House was a building that, had it been contemplated years later after the passage in 1970 of Vermont's Act 250, might never have come into being. The environmental-protection law, which over the years has been a thorn in the side of many ski-resort developers, places a high premium on ecological sensitivity and puts any development above 2,500 feet under

Opposite: The terrain from the gondola—first opened in 1968—gave Stowe something it previously lacked: long, wide intermediate runs. Below: The smooth contours of runs like Perry Merrill allow groomers to produce an excellent skiing surface.

particularly close scrutiny. Purely from a developer's perspective, Starr's and Ruschp's timing couldn't have been better.

In short, the gondola, the Cliff House and the terrain offered an attractive package to the casual, fair-weather skier: easy cruising terrain; sun; a fast, weather-shielding lift, taking skiers from bottom to top in 10 minutes; and a good restaurant with a good view. The two main runs, Perry Merrill and Gondolier, essentially represented intermediate nirvana.

However, the four-passenger gondola, the centerpiece of a two-year, $1.5 million improvement program, got off to an inauspicious start when it first opened in December 1968. On New Year's Eve, one of the gondola cars fell off the cable, crashing 20 feet below and seriously injuring one passenger. The accident received wide media attention throughout New England—not exactly the kind of publicity the resort was hoping to generate with its new pet project.

At the same time, the resort fell upon a stroke of good luck to help mollify anxieties about the gondola's initial shortcomings. Snow in the winter of 1968-69 came early and kept coming, resulting, by March 15, in a settled snowpack of 147 inches at the snow stake on the mountain. In the Mt. Mansfield Ski Club newsletter, Bill Harrington, the club's president at the time, wrote: "This winter will be remembered for many years to come with its record-breaking snow depth, no January thaw, no long stretches of windy or 25-below-zero weather, just a good long season of skiing!" Charlie Lord concurred in his annual analysis of snow conditions on the mountain, writing of the winter of 1968-69: "It can be said, without reservation, that this season

was the best ever in the last 35 years." It is an axiom in the world of skiing that all tribulations can be expelled by a good snow year.

Meanwhile Spruce Peak, which never quite fulfilled the original vision of Starr and Ruschp, was perhaps saved by snowmaking, first installed in 1967. Over time, Spruce began to find its niche, largely as a place for ski instruction, and its glory years may still lie ahead, thanks to a 10-year development plan now in the works (see page 101). Because the Spruce slopes haven't been heavily graded, the natural contours provide a series of stepped-up challenges ideal in helping beginners advance quickly to a higher level of skiing, adds Steve Jones. "It's a great place to learn how to ski," says Jones, an instructor for more than 20 years at Stowe. "It's a place where people can learn about skiing

real terrain, not just on runs dictated by what engineers said."

Spruce has also come into its own as the warm respite from the cold of Mt. Mansfield on particularly frigid days. "It sure is a nice place to go on a cold afternoon when Mt. Mansfield is crowded," says Charlie Adams. "You look over at Mansfield on those brutally cold days and it's in the shade, and you just feel for all those poor people."

And finally, with more and more skiers and snowboarders venturing into the woods on Mt. Mansfield in search of adventure, Spruce has become the exploratory zone for the off-trail avant-garde. Areas like Birthday Bowl, on the northwest shoulder of Sterling Mountain (the backside of Big Spruce), have become the province of those seeking a more private off-trail escape than popular Mt. Mansfield now allows. "Big Spruce is

Opposite: Sepp Ruschp was reluctant at first to invest heavily in snowmaking, but competition from resorts like Killington forced his hand in 1967. Right: Trees on Spruce Peak coated with machine-made snow.

an undiscovered gem," says Adams, referring mostly to the off-trail skiing. "For many of the really hardcore guys, that's their terrain up there."

The hardcore guys are all over the woods these days, both on Mt. Mansfield and Spruce Peak. Off-trail skiing at Stowe has seen an explosion in popularity since the mid 1990s. That's a trend that concerns environmentalists and the ski area's safety personnel, who see a greatly increased potential for environmental damage and serious injury (see Chapter 5). It also worries long-time Stowe skiers, who see once-secret stashes in the woods so heavily skied that moguls have begun appearing in places between the trees.

Still, as Jay Bowen says, there's a lot of territory to explore; once the off-trail opportunities are drawn into the equation, the

skiing experience at Stowe expands exponentially. "Take a trail and multiply it by 10," says Bowen. "You've got that many 'trails' in between trails."

It is an unofficial trail network that breeds its own subculture. You know you have gained entry into the inner circle when you know all the names, bequeathed by word of mouth among local skiers and snowboarders, of the many lines through the trees: Angel Food, Goat Woods, Beast of the East, the Planets and so on. And you know you have arrived at the subversive extreme of the subculture when you are one of the "gardeners" or "whittlers" who "maintain" tree lines by illegally clearing brush and small trees in the summertime, to the consternation of state foresters. It is a blatantly illicit activity, but it is also an activity, with a long tradition at Stowe, that is almost impossible to police.

There is more to the off-trail bounty than just tree skiing, too. The entire mountain, with all of its terrain varieties and complexities, comes into play. "The whole thing begins with the Chin," says Adams, referring to Mt. Mansfield's craggy, above-timberline highpoint. "The Chin is a big-mountain adventure in Vermont."

To get there requires about a 20-minute hike from the Cliff House, and once there, you're in a rawly beautiful environment of green, lichen-covered rocks, tundral growth, wind-scoured snow and ice, with a view in all directions to New Hampshire, Canada and New York. Through seams in the rocks, small chutes and mini-couloirs descend, such as Hourglass, Profanity and North Ridge. And when snow conditions are particularly favorable, as they were in the winter of 2000-01,

more extreme terrain along the summit ridge becomes skiable: the Kitchen Wall, 100-Inch Chute and other lines with similarly daunting names. It is skiing as unforgiving as it is alluring to high-end skiers and snowboarders. As Bowen says, "It's not like the West, where you've got all those safety bail-out zones. You've got to be on top of it with every turn, and if you go down, you get hurt."

These sluices of snow and ice lead within about 600 vertical feet into groves of gnarled, high-elevation spruce trees, severely stunted in their growth or reduced to lifeless carcasses, ravaged by the brutal weather that often crashes into the Mt. Mansfield summit. Bowen refers to such trees as "Green Mountain cactuses," with spiked, broken branches that can impale any person making an unplanned close encounter. And once beyond the conifer

zone, the descent leads into the hardwood forests of maple, beech and birch that are so quintessentially Vermont. For all of the big-mountain thrills that the Chin might render, it is the whimsical, almost dancelike experience through the tight corridors and muted light of the lower-elevation hardwoods that raises local sentiment to the threshold of rhapsody.

"It just takes you away," says Jones, of skiing in the trees on a powder day. "If you're a good skier, you never forget it. It affects your soul."

Perhaps so. But if you were to look for the ultimate Stowe ski run, you'd probably look for some combination of on-trail and off-trail terrain, a run that harkens back to the exploratory nature of Stowe skiing in its earliest years. Stu Campbell remembers one particular run with Charlie Lord several years ago, shortly before Lord died.

"It was an unseasonably cold spring day following a warm spell," Campbell recalls. "The snow was all frozen coral heads, and the wind was blowing. People were sitting in the lodge, and no one wanted to go out. But Charlie came up to me at the [ski-school] desk and said, 'Let's go skiing.'

"We took a route I couldn't possibly repeat in a million years. Charlie would find a patch of corn snow that was just right in the sun; then he'd cut through the trees to another perfect patch of corn. We kept going like that. And when we got to the bottom, we were grinning ear to ear, while everyone else was bitching."

The master, Lord, in his workshop—proving that Stowe skiing, in all of its multifaceted complexity, is not just what it is, but also whatever you are willing to make of it. ⊠

111

On the summit ridge of Mt. Mansfield. Before hiking into the
backcountry, say environmental experts, wait until the snow depth
is sufficient to protect delicate vegetation.

CHAPTER 5

Beyond Boundaries

P rofanity. Hourglass. North Ridge. Hellbrook. The Bruce. Tear Drop. To a small but growing corps of Stowe skiers and snowboarders, these names echo with a reverential resonance—sacred places in the temple of Mt. Mansfield backcountry skiing. Among Eastern ski areas, Stowe is the acknowledged leader of the pack when it comes to off-trail exploration.

This, in large part, must be attributed to Mt. Mansfield's unique terrain: the above-timberline summit of the Chin, where seams in the rock collect deep pockets of snow; the deep mountainside gouges like Hellbrook, a bobsled run through the woods; the well-spaced trees where snow lies shielded from sun and wind; the old trails like the Bruce or Tear Drop, "ghost trails," as they are sometimes called, dating back to the origins of Stowe skiing, now partially overgrown but still eminently skiable. No amalgam of backcountry terrain in New England is more inviting.

At the same time, the deep passion among Stowe skiers and snowboarders for venturing off-trail also reflects an atavistic connection with the original Stowe skiers, who explored the mountain before there were trails. There is, simply, a long-running tradition in Stowe, passed along from one generation to the next, for this sort of behavior.

Still, this is a very different era than that of the early 1930s. Today, with lifts providing quick access to most of the best off-trail caches, long and arduous hiking is no longer a necessary part of the backcountry equation. Equipment today is vastly different. Snowboards are able to adroitly navigate through tight corridors through the trees; wider, shorter skis can surf effortlessly over deep wind-deposited snow. The hiking is minimal and the skiing, at least compared with that of the 1930s, is relatively easy, opening up the backcountry to a much broader population.

As a result, backcountry skiing and snowboarding on Mt. Mansfield had, by the turn of the millennium, increased significantly, according to a number of people who keep track of such things. And as off-trail exploration has risen, a host of legal, political, environmental and cultural concerns have come into play—stuff that the pioneers of the 1930s never contemplated.

The skiers who explored the mountains in the 1930s before there were trails simply hiked up and skied down wherever they felt like it. They weren't saddled with the weight of the potential animosities and cultural clashes that those venturing off-trail today must take into consideration.

Backcountry skiing and snowboarding on Mt. Mansfield today is framed foremost by the complex and sometimes disputed

issue of stewardship. Who is in charge on the mountain? Who has the right to decide what usage is most appropriate? Who determines what balance is acceptable between environmental preservation and recreational activity, or between environmental preservation and development?

Several parties, each with some sort of rightful claim, throw their hats into the stewardship ring, and rarely do their priorities dovetail seamlessly. Stowe Mountain Resort, the Green Mountain Club, the state's Agency of Natural Resources, the University of Vermont, the skiers and snowboarders themselves, the ski patrol and search-and-rescue teams, along with various peripherally interested parties—all invest some sort of interest in the way Mt. Mansfield's backcountry is used. Conflicts have become inevitable, although for the most part the various parties seem to have made an effort to fold their differences into a workable truce, no matter how uneasy it might be at times.

The state of Vermont is by far the largest landholder and as such has a powerful voice in the backcountry debate. In 1914, the state acquired 5,000 acres on the mountain, a parcel that is part of the much larger state-owned Mt. Mansfield State Forest, covering 40,000 acres in all. Most of the ski-resort terrain is on state land. The state government—in this case, the Agency of Natural Resources, a part of Vermont's Department of Forests, Parks and Recreation—is charged with the responsibility of assuring that the land be used in the best interests of the state's people. That's not always an easy mandate, particularly when economic, environmental and recreational considerations come into conflict.

Exploring the summit ridge beyond ski-trail boundaries is not a recent invention. A skier in the 1930s works his way through the trees toward the Summit House, the mountaintop hotel that stood from 1858 until 1964.

Through a curious historical twist, the University of Vermont (UVM) owns 400 acres on the summit ridge of the mountain. In 1859, William Henry Harrison Bingham, the tourism impresario who happened to own a good deal of land on the mountain in the mid 19th century, sold the summit to the university for $1,000. Bingham, whose finances were occasionally stretched thin by his entrepreneurial zeal, conducted the transaction as a means of raising cash for various projects—the Summit House and the Mt. Mansfield Hotel, for example.

But with some preservational foresight, he deeded the land to the university with the restrictive wording that the land only be used for "scientific purposes." This would assure that the summit of Vermont's most impressive mountain—and Bingham's most valuable tourist attraction—would remain undeveloped.

Exactly how the term "scientific purposes" should be interpreted, however, has been the subject of considerable date in the ensuing century and a half. It has been up to the university to decide, as Rick Paradis of UVM's School of Natural Resources puts it, "whether to interpret the deed literally or liberally." In permitting considerable recreational usage on its land, both in summer and in winter, the university has chosen over the years to be fairly liberal in its interpretation.

While it owns no land on Mt. Mansfield, the Green Mountain Club (GMC) manages and maintains the Long Trail, which passes over the mountain's summit. The venerable 265-mile trail, built between 1910 and 1930, follows the Green Mountain spine from Massachusetts to the Canadian border. Older even than the Appalachian Trail, for which it was consid-

The Cult of the Trees

On the whole, they're probably older than you might expect. Many are in their 40s, others in their 50s, some in their 60s—"recycled teenagers," in the words of one tree-skiing elder statesman. They've been at it for four decades or more, beginning in the late 1960s. "We would all meet at the top, smoke pot, then go off and do our thing in the trees," recalls one long-time tree skier.

There might be talk of the number of off-trail skiers and snowboarders growing dramatically, swollen by the increased interest in something more adventurous than mainstream trail skiing. But the real core group of tree skiers remains relatively small and relatively advanced in age, primarily because the refined art of off-trail skiing at Stowe—where to go, when to go, how to navigate the tight lines through the trees—takes time to learn. There is no guidebook, no map, no instruction manual. Knowledge is passed along by word of mouth, sparingly, and even word of mouth isn't particularly reliable.

"Many among the core group don't want people to know about this stuff," says Steve Jones, who has been skiing the Mt. Mansfield woods for more than 30 years. "They really protect their domain and don't like giving away secrets. It's like fishing: You might tell people where your favorite fishing hole is, but you might just as likely tell them where it isn't." They become irked when articles in national magazines reveal formerly secret locations, and their private stashes are suddenly overrun.

They belong, says off-trail regular Kim Brown, to "an early-morning culture." On a day dawning with particular promise, the inner circle begins gathering at the base of the quad chair on Mt. Mansfield as early as 6:30, in preparation for the 7:30 lift opening. They know that in a place like Stowe, with so many good skiers who know the mountain well, that the best lines won't remain untracked for long. From the top of the lift, they fan out into the woods with an almost military, guerrilla-like precision, taking care, in a kind of tacit understanding, that no skier steals the line of another.

They also approach off-trail skiing with an almost military preparedness. "Tele skis, fat skis, ice skis—whatever the conditions are, they're ready for it," says Jones. "And they don't let the weather bother them, because they know how to dress." They're both accommodating and skeptical of the new wave of skiers and snowboarders venturing into the woods. "A lot of these younger kids don't have the survival skills," says Jones, also noting that some of the less proficient snowboarders tend to scrape away fresh snow by sideslipping through tight spots, an egregious off-trail faux pas. Nevertheless, Jones insists, "We're accepting of them. They're part of the program."

After a particularly good day, the core of the core is apt to come together at a place like the Matterhorn, the popular watering hole a couple of miles down the Mountain Road. It is here, says Jones, that the names of lines through the trees are often born. "The names get created over beer," says Jones. "Somebody comes up with a really cool name, and if it's good enough, it sticks." And so Angel Food and the Planets and Kitchen Wall are born, never to be found on any official trail map. They exist only in the minds and experience of the core group, where the devotion for tree skiing runs as thick and deep as the woods themselves.

Left: You won't find it on any trail map, and few Stowe locals will openly divulge their favorite, off-trail powder stashes. Opposite: A hiker on the Long Trail on Mt. Mansfield. Although winter back-country use is increasing rapidly, the high-mountain environment is more vulnerable in summer, when trail use is much heavier.

ered a model, the Long Trail is an honored institution within the national hiking community. As a result, the Green Mountain Club carries significant clout into the Mt. Mansfield backcountry debate.

Then, there is the ski resort, operating as a commercial enterprise on state land through a 10-year renewable lease. As in any landlord-tenant arrangement, the resort must keep its landlord's interests—the state's interests—in mind, operating responsibly in accordance with the mandate of the state to act in the best interests of its citizens. The lease defines the resort's responsibilities in fairly general terms: to promote and develop winter sport, and also "to provide for the public good and benefit."

This wording leaves considerable room for interpretive leeway. Most of the land within the resort's leased area is not devel-

oped; fewer than 300 of 1,400 leased acres have been developed for designated trails. The rest is forested, and as off-trail skiing enthusiast Kim Brown points out, "much of the best woods skiing is between the trails within the perimeter of the ski area." The extent of the resort's responsibility on this undeveloped land, particularly in terms of aiding lost and injured skiers, is somewhat ambiguous.

Rob Apple, the resort's director of planning and development, declares without hesitation that "we have no liabilities out there. You go out there and you're on your own. There's nothing in the lease that requires us to do anything," in terms of managing off-trail usage.

Maybe so. But liability is one thing, ethical responsibility another. As Apple readily admits, the resort's ski patrol is

inevitably obliged, ethically if not legally, to assist people in trouble. "Are we required to go in?" asks Apple about off-trail rescue. "No. Will we go? Yes." If someone is in trouble in the woods within the resort's leased area, the ski patrol obviously cannot simply ignore the problem.

As a result, while the resort permits off-trail exploration, it tries to steer clear of promoting it, despite the inherent marketing appeal of untracked snow in dramatic backcountry settings. In recent years, the resort's ski patrol has been drawn into well-documented off-trail rescue efforts that have been both time-consuming and dangerous, discouraging the resort from exacerbating the problem by making public gestures condoning backcountry exploration. As Apple says, "individuals have the right, at their own risk, to explore the Vermont woods. But the resort doesn't endorse it."

This policy echoes the frontline view taken by other principals in the backcountry debate. "[Off-trail skiing] is something we neither encourage or discourage," says Mike Fraysier of the state's Agency of Natural Resources. Those words, "neither encourage or discourage," recur with almost mantric repetition in any discussion of winter backcountry usage. No one wants to promote it; no one wants to prohibit it.

While the various mountain stewards might differ in their opinions on what backcountry behavior on Mt. Mansfield is acceptable, they do agree on one thing: Winter backcountry usage has risen significantly in recent years. "Winter use is clearly increasing," says Ben Rose, executive director of the Green Mountain Club.

Left: Some backcountry glades are formed naturally, by rockslides and avalanches, though so-called "gardeners" sometimes assist nature by illegally clearing brush and saplings. Opposite: Environmentalists are concerned about the increased traffic on the Chin, which can attract a crowd on a powder day.

UVM's Rick Paradis talks of "literally hundreds of folks on the Chin" on days when snow and weather conditions are particularly favorable.

These reports come within the context of a boom in the popularity of off-trail tree skiing at the end of the 1990s, in Stowe as elsewhere throughout the East. It has become an inside joke in the Stowe skiing community that on the day after a storm, after powder on designated trails has been tracked out, that the trails are virtually deserted. Local skiers and snowboarders head for the woods, for well-hidden stashes of untracked snow. There are, says Kim Brown, "hundreds and hundreds of people skiing out of bounds on this mountain."

There is nothing either wrong or illegal in doing so, but it does raise concerns. "I'm not worried that the numbers are increasing, but that the level of awareness is not increasing," says Neil Van Dyke of the Stowe Hazardous Terrain Evacuation Team (see page 125), a nonprofit group that rescues people who are lost or injured in the region's backcountry.

Van Dyke is referring primarily to awareness of the safety issues inherent in off-trail skiing. "What concerns me," he says, "is that too many people aren't approaching this as a backcountry experience. They think they're just going skiing, just a little bit off the trail, and not backcountry skiing."

In other words, say Van Dyke and other safety experts, too many skiers and snowboarders head off-trail without the proper safety equipment or a full understanding of the moods and dangers of the uncontrolled winter environment they might be entering. Ideally, even when taking a seemingly benign run through

the trees between trails, any off-trail traveler should carry a pack with such essentials as first-aid gear, extra clothing, food, water, a whistle and even a cell phone. But only a minority of even the most experienced off-trail skiers and riders on Mt. Mansfield are so well equipped. And many misjudge how easy it is to get lost in the woods and how hard it is to be found. Stories abound of lost skiers or snowboarders, purblind to the hazards of the backcountry in winter, being rescued after spending a night lost in the woods. Sometimes they are found within shouting distance of a designated trail.

The lack of awareness is not due to a lack of information. A clear warning is printed on the resort's trail map: "If you leave the open and designated ski trails, you are entering areas that have no first aid or rescue services. By Vermont statute, you can-

not expect any help regarding your actions in these areas." Signs around the ski area post similar admonitions. A sign along the main hiking trail leading from the top of the gondola to the Chin reads: "THIS IS AN UNPATROLLED AREA WITH UNMARKED OBSTACLES, SEVERE CONDITIONS AND DANGEROUS PRECIPICES. PLEASE DO NOT PROCEED IF YOU ARE ALONE, UNPREPARED OR UNCERTAIN."

Brown believes that winter backcountry users on Mt. Mansfield are at least somewhat more aware of the potential hazards they might encounter than summer users are. Indeed, it is probably fair to say that most of the off-trail skiers on Mt. Mansfield are committed backcountry enthusiasts with at least some knowledge of proper backcountry behavior, a characterization that is less certain among the hundreds of hikers who use the

Ice and heavy snow can turn trees, particularly supple birch trees, into drooping, low-hanging obstacles in the backcountry. Experienced back-country skiers carry a pack with proper safety gear whenever leaving the trail network.

The Stowe Hazardous Terrain Evacuation Team

The conditions on the Chin were ferocious: Snow blowing, wind roaring at about 50 miles an hour, visibility zero, the dark of night all consuming. The conditions were so bad, says Neil Van Dyke, chief of the Stowe Hazardous Terrain Evacuation Team, that "people [on the team] were literally blown off the mountain," knocked off their feet and down on the ice and rock of the Chin by the force of the wind.

It was January 1998, and the team was searching for three skiers reported missing on the mountain. Two brothers from Montpelier, Vermont, and a teenager from Pennsylvania had met on top of the Chin that day. They then made the mistake of skiing down the western side of the mountain, away from the ski resort and toward Underhill. "The history on Mt. Mansfield is that most of the time, they [lost skiers] end up on the Underhill side," says Van Dyke. "We usually assign a higher probability on that side when we search."

The search continued through the night and into the next morning, with close to 100 people, led by Van Dyke's 12-member team, joining in the effort. By morning, the Vermont National Guard was called in as well, with a helicopter to aid in the search. And late in the morning, the three lost skiers were finally found: One was seen hiking on a road toward Underhill; the two others, scrambling through a stream drainage above Underhill, were located by spotters in the helicopter.

They had suffered from mild hypothermia but were otherwise all right.

The Stowe Hazardous Terrain Evacuation Team is manned by a group of highly skilled outdoorspeople. They are accomplished climbers, backcountry skiers, first-aid specialists and generally people willing to put themselves in potentially life-threatening situations, for minimal pay, in order to save lives. They know what they're doing. In their more than 20-year history, their winter record is impeccable; the survival rate of lost or injured victims on Mt. Mansfield has been 100 percent.

But this is not a winter-only operation or one focused solely on the search for lost skiers. Some of the team's most difficult rescues have been on the cliffs of Smugglers' Notch, in rescuing stranded rock climbers or ice climbers mangled by falling slabs of ice. It is in the Notch, says Van Dyke, where the team has encountered its only fatalities. It is in the Notch where Van Dyke himself nearly died while trying to rescue a stranded father and son. He fell 60 feet onto a rock-strewn slope, and was fortunate to survive with only broken ribs, a punctured lung and a broken wrist.

So why, through sleepless nights and savage weather and life-threatening danger at the paltry pay rate of $8 an hour, do they bother? "It's the feeling you get when you rescue someone," says Van Dyke. "It's a great sense of relief and accomplishment. That's why you do it."

This is an unpatrolled area with unmarked obstacles, severe conditions, and dangerous precipices. Please do not proceed if you are alone, unprepared, or uncertain.

mountain trails in summer. "On average, a person in winter has a higher level of understanding of putting themselves in a hostile, Arctic environment," Brown says.

Maybe so, and no doubt the local corps of off-trail skiers to which Brown belongs scores high marks in backcountry awareness. At the same time, winter brings into play a whole set of potentially life-threatening consequences—exposure, frostbite and even avalanches—not encountered in summer. If winter travelers are, on average, better informed, they also need to be better prepared. And clearly not everyone in the growing contingent of off-trail adventurers is fully up to the task.

How, then, can off-trail skiing on Mt. Mansfield be made safer? In some ways, the simplest solution might be to ban backcountry skiing on Mt. Mansfield. "It would be an easy answer:

put up a chain-link fence and close off the backcountry," says Van Dyke. The Stowe Hazardous Terrain Evacuation Team must perform several complex and often dangerous search-and-rescue operations on the mountain every winter. Closing the backcountry would take care of that problem.

But it is not a realistic answer, if for no other reason than it would be a public-relations nightmare. As the Green Mountain Club's Ben Rose says, "If you try to prohibit it [backcountry use], you're perceived as exclusionary." UVM's Rick Paradis agrees. "We've entertained the idea in the past [of closing off the Chin to skiers]. But it's just an idea we floated, and people resisted strongly. They would ask, 'Who made you the authority?'"

Most of the principals agree that better and more extensive signage, warning of the hazards of off-trail travel, would help

reduce the number of unprepared skiers heading into the backcountry. As a deterrent, the resort has also instituted a policy—similar to those at many North American resorts—charging victims for the cost of off-trail or out-of-bounds rescue. That cost can frequently run into the thousands of dollars, and even experienced off-trail skiers like Brown agree that the policy is reasonable. But it is inherently problematic, too. Rescuers, after all, are ethically obliged to help out lost or injured people regardless of their ability or willingness to pay. And once someone has been rescued, it can be difficult to collect payment after the fact.

Ultimately, the answer to maximizing winter backcountry safety is probably in efforts to educate and inform. "There's been a strong push to make people aware of the hazards, to get the message of responsibility out there," says Brown. "You need backcountry knowledge, you need to be technically strong, and you need to be aware that you're putting yourself in a hostile winter environment." Unfortunately, as winter exploration on the mountain increases, it is probably safe to assume that an increasing number of backcountry travelers will fail to meet Brown's high standards of skill, backcountry savvy and awareness.

Karen Wagner, the resort's risk manager for mountain operations, concurs: "We're concerned about people with lesser skills taking on bigger challenges. I can't believe some of the places I see tracks in Smugglers' Notch. Our ski patrol does between 10 and 12 off-trail rescues a year. So far, we haven't had any fatalities, but there have been some really close calls."

The Mt. Mansfield summit is essentially an Arctic environment, and home to the largest community of Arctic-tundra vegetation in Vermont. Among the wildflowers that bloom in summer is the rare Diapensia lapponica (above), a "true alpine species," according to one expert. Opposite: The backcountry environment is especially vulnerable when the snow cover is thin.

If safety is the foremost concern among people like Van Dyke and the Mt. Mansfield ski patrol, environmental issues are front and center for most others in the backcountry debate. The question, in simplest terms, is: What impact has the increase in off-trail exploration had on Mt. Mansfield's environmental health?

The answer is that nobody knows for sure. No comprehensive studies have been done, and as UVM's Rick Paradis admits, "the jury is still out on the level of impact." By Paradis' estimate, based primarily on observation, "there has been a moderate amount of damage." The university is concerned, of course, with impacts primarily on its land, the summit ridge, which is home to a number of rare Arctic plants. Moss, lichen and ground-creeping wildflowers grow on and between rocks. Diapensia lap-

ponica, for example, is what UVM's Rick Paradis describes as a "true Alpine species that grows on exposed, windswept ridges." Because of the harsh climate, the maturation cycle of these slow-growing plants is extremely long. Even a small amount of damage can require years of remedial regeneration.

These species are not the sort of plants that skiers and snowboarders, hiking up the Chin, would probably notice. But as Paradis says, "If this area is being trampled by summit seekers, there is no doubt these species will decline."

Still, the university remains reluctant to prohibit skiers and snowboarders from hiking up to the Chin. It would be hard, after all, to justify a policy allowing summer hikers on the summit and banning skiers and snowboarders in winter. And any efforts to ban both summer and winter use would undoubtedly be greeted

with a firestorm of protest. So the debate is not whether winter use should be permitted, but rather how it should best be managed.

People like Paradis and Ben Rose offer a few guidelines in the name of self-imposed responsibility. For example, says Rose, off-trail skiing "is not an early-season activity." Skiers and snowboarders, he says, should wait until the snow is sufficiently deep, both on the summit and in the woods, to provide protection for ground-level vegetation. According to Paradis, studies in the White Mountains of New Hampshire have suggested that a snowpack of between 12 and 18 inches is probably sufficient to provide a basic layer of protection. "If there is ample snowpack," he says, "there should be little impact to sensitive vegetation." Indeed, he says, there is a much more pronounced effort to keep hikers on trails in the summer, when the vegetation is more exposed to potential damage.

Still, snow, particularly at high and exposed elevations, rarely lies in a neat, uniform blanket. Even when the general snowpack on the Mt. Mansfield summit is several feet deep, the effects of wind and sun can strip away snow and leave vegetation vulnerable. So Rose issues a simpler guideline: "If your edges can cut vegetation, don't go." But even this might be an inadequate gauge, because as Paradis notes, more damage is usually done on the ascent than the descent. So Rose's axiom needs a corollary: If your boots can trample vegetation, don't go.

In the past, efforts have been made to establish a "herd path," marked by stakes, that all of those climbing the Chin would use. But the strategy has proved only moderately effective. In addition to difficulties in keeping the trail-marking stakes in place, there is little assurance that all climbers will use the route.

A powder day on the Forehead of Mt. Mansfield. The Chin looms over the Cliff House in the distance.

Another possible solution contemplated by the Green Mountain Club and the University of Vermont has been hiring a full-time winter caretaker to oversee activity along the summit ridge. Caretakers regularly watch over the summit during busy summer hiking months. But in addition to the expense of paying somebody, the idea of a winter caretaker has intrinsic drawbacks. Not only would some kind of shelter need to be built to house a prospective caretaker, but few are the individuals willing to spend long, lonely hours in the harsh climate of Vermont's highest mountain in winter.

Winter activity in the forests below the summit raises a different set of issues that have sparked considerable controversy among backcountry users and environmentalists. The specific focus of controversy is illicit trail clearing: the sur-

reptitious removal of brush and small trees by local skiers and snowboarders to create more open lines through the woods. It is, as Mike Fraysier of the Agency of Natural Resources says simply, "an illegal activity that we are strongly discouraging."

That is not, however, a policy that sits well with many local skiers and snowboarders. The clearing of brush and saplings is something skiers have been doing on Mt. Mansfield for years. It is ingrained in Stowe's long-standing culture of off-trail skiing. Those who continue to clear lines through the woods, despite the threat of prosecution, argue that their activity is not just benign; in some cases, they say, it might actually be beneficial to the health of the forest. The clearing of noxious brush and small growth can be a way of promoting the growth of healthier trees.

The scofflaw cutters are also, according to Brown, careful to

Hellbrook

Among devoted Stowe skiers, it is the alpha and omega of backcountry skiing, Mt. Mansfield's defining off-trail experience. Hellbrook is a special place and not just because of its inherent challenge or deep-woods beauty or the snow that sifts abundantly through the trees. Hellbrook, says long-time Stowe skier and ski instructor Steve Jones, "is sensual skiing."

It is also difficult skiing. As Jay Bowen, another Stowe regular says, "the most impressive thing to me is the entrance. When you hike it in the summer, you really understand how steep it is. You can't believe it can be skied." In summer, it is a hiking trail that runs along the cascading, eponymous brook. But in winter, when the brook freezes solid and the sharp contours of the terrain are smoothed over with snow, it becomes the most renowned tree run in Stowe.

So widespread is its fame that Kim Brown, a leading advocate of off-trail skiing in Stowe, remembers overhearing a conversation on the tram in Snowbird, Utah, a favorite hangout of hardcore skiers. Two skiers were discussing their favorite runs of all time. "As I listened," says Brown, "I realized the run one guy was talking about was an amazing day on Hellbrook."

Of course, popularity can have its drawbacks. Search-and-rescuers and environmentalists are not the only ones concerned about overuse of Hellbrook; skiers and snowboarders are, too. "Five years ago, Hellbrook was a local secret," says Bowen. "Now just about everybody who has a season pass tries it at least once a year."

Still, says Bowen, "it's always worth the hike for whatever you get out of it. It's always changing in there. I remember skiing it early in the season, when there was no real base [of snow] to cover the ground. When we got down, we looked back up and saw dirt and leaves where our tracks were. But while skiing it, we just floated down, never hitting anything. It is a magical place."

avoid environmentally sensitive areas and species. "None of us wants to cut above the 2,500-foot level," he says, referring to the conifer forests above 2,500 feet on the mountain, where the potential harm of illicit trail cutting is greatest. "We want to work only in the drainages and hardwood forests [at lower levels.]"

Fraysier, however, is not sympathetic. Mt. Mansfield's forests, he says, are public land, on which it is the state's responsibility to develop a forestry management plan in the best interests of all of Vermont's people. "It's everybody's property, not the property of the extreme-skiing community," he says. Furthermore, he says, the surreptitious cutting may not be in keeping with the state's comprehensive forest-management plan.

Right: The treeline on Mt. Mansfield is at approximately 4,000 feet. Just below that level, stunted spruce trees can produce a route-finding challenge. Opposite: When conditions are right, the thrills of the backcountry are hard to beat.

In addition, says Rob Apple, there has been evidence of cutting above 2,500 feet, despite Brown's assertions to the contrary. Of particular concern is the potential impact on the habitat of the Bicknell's thrush, a rare bird species that lives in the high-elevation forests. (In fact, possible damage to the thrush's habitat has been a stumbling block in a number of recently proposed expansions at other ski resorts in New England.) While Brown and other backcountry veterans might consider themselves conscientious backcountry citizens, Apple asserts that the interest in off-trail skiing has spurred "an increase in the number of people who aren't [environmentally] sensitive."

Of course, policing thousands of acres of forested land is almost impossible. Rare is the case in which an illicit trail clearer is caught in the act and prosecuted. So the state, through warn-

ings and information programs, can do little more than fire shots across the bow of the trail-clearing community, hoping in the process to keep the activity to a minimum. In the summer of 2002, one illicit cutter ("who was very contrite and apologetic," according to Fraysier) was required, as part of his punishment, to write a letter to the local paper admitting his culpability and condemning the practice. But exactly how much impact such small measures will have in discouraging others from clearing trails in the woods is dubious.

With various groups with diverse recreational interests coming together on Mt. Mansfield in winter, a clash of cultures is inevitable. As Vermont's largest mountain, Mansfield commands attention from a wide array of interested parties: skiers, hikers,

ecologists, geologists, meteorologists, biologists and so on. As such, it can often become as much a battleground as a playground, a place in which various groups seek, philosophically and politically, to take a stand.

In particular, the hiking community and the downhill-skiing community have long regarded each other with a wariness that sometimes boils over into outright scorn. "The GMC hikers think they're somewhat superior to skiers because we ride up on lifts," says Brown. "They don't think we're quite as in tune with the environment as they are." Meanwhile, the Green Mountain Club claims that skiers and snowboarders not only abuse the Long Trail (where downhill skiing is prohibited) but also lack sensitivity toward others—snowshoers and touring backcountry skiers—who might be on the mountain in winter.

The GMC's Rose, for example, complains about reports of "airborne snowboarders" and "near misses" between off-trail skiers and other travelers in the woods in winter. "I wouldn't want to take my kids showshoeing up Hellbrook on weekends," he says. As off-trail traffic increases, he says, "we could see something tragic at some point."

Uneasiness also colors the relationship between the ski resort and the University of Vermont. As a large commercial enterprise that literally attracts thousands of people to the mountain during busy winter days, the resort is a broad-sided target for environmental criticism. Even if there is a mandate in the resort's lease "to promote winter recreation," some critics believe that the resort oversteps its bounds, particularly regarding the promotion of off-trail activity.

"They [the resort's management] are often of two voices," says Paradis. "At times, they appear to be discouraging [off-trail skiing]. Yet they are also promoting it." Paradis points specifically to photos in recent resort brochures of skiers and boarders descending the Chin in gloriously deep powder and abundant sunshine. Such alluring imagery, say Paradis and others, is not in keeping with the spirit of neither encouraging nor discouraging off-trail skiing.

Discussions on such matters have at times been heated. And with a large, long-range development plan in the works, the resort has found itself under increasing scrutiny from the Green Mountain Club, UVM and the state to behave with environmental prudence and circumspection.

Still, efforts are being made to work together, to create what Rose calls "a cooperative partnership to manage the impacts on Mt.

Mansfield." And despite the alarms sounded about dramatic increases in off-trail activity, the fact remains that those who venture from designated trails represent a very small minority of skiers. "I think the worst is over," says Rose. "I'm not convinced that the problem is going to continue to grow geometrically."

Indeed, according to Rose, the GMC is much more concerned throughout the state about motorized vehicles rather than backcountry skiers—snowmobiles and off-road vehicles that may be using or crossing hiking trails recklessly. There is little question that a snowmobile, irresponsibly deployed in the backcountry, can cause far more damage than either a skier or a snowshoer.

The basics are in place to ensure that off-trail exploration on Mt. Mansfield in winter remains relatively safe and environmentally

Left: The Chin in its winter mantle of rime ice and snow. High winds often scour the summit when harsh, winter storms hit. Snow stripped by wind from the summit gets deposited lower on the mountain in the trees (opposite), where knowledgeable Stowe locals say the best backcountry skiing is found.

harmless. Warning signs have been posted on the mountain. The law against cutting brush and saplings is clear. The guidelines for safe backcountry travel (bring the proper equipment, never go alone, etc.) are simple and very learnable. Organizations like the Green Mountain Club and the Vermont Institute of Natural Science continue to push education efforts promoting proper backcountry behavior.

And perhaps most important, there is word of mouth—passing from one skier to the next almost organically, as if through a common bloodstream—that informs the backcountry enthusiasts of Stowe. Meetings in coffee shops for updates on prevailing snow conditions; the passing on of backcountry lore from old pros like Brown to the next generation of off-trail novitiates; a shared familiarity with the ripples and contours of the mountain:

It all belongs to a Stowe tradition spanning generations.

Backcountry skiers in Stowe are well aware that their actions are being scrutinized by the state, the resort, the Green Mountain Club, the university and the search-and-rescue specialists. They don't want to see this beautiful thing they've got—arguably the best off-trail skiing in New England—wrecked by a few people behaving stupidly. And so they do what they can to make sure the word passes on: Be smart. Be safe. And respect the environment, even if it might mean, when scrutinizing backs are turned, clearing vexatious underbrush that might interfere with a great line of powder skiing through the trees. For as attuned as they might be to the rules and traditions of the backcountry, in their pursuit of the best off-trail experience possible, even the most conscientious backcountry skiers are not without sin. ◪

Billy Kidd moved with his family from Burlington, Vermont, to Stowe,
where he became a top junior racer in the 1950s.

CHAPTER 6

A Racing Legacy

For a young Billy Kidd, it must have been like being a teenage basketball hopeful given a chance to play a little one-on-one with Michael Jordan. It was the late 1950s, and Kidd's heroes—ski-racing legends like Austrians Toni Sailer and Anderl Molterer—were in Stowe to compete in the American International, one of the most prestigious racing events in the country at the time. Sepp Ruschp, president of the Mt. Mansfield Company, wanted the world's best competitors to be there, and C.V. Starr, Stowe's wealthy owner, came up with the money to make sure it would happen.

Kidd was a young hotshot, a guy who would go on to win a silver medal in the Olympic slalom in 1964. But in the late 1950s, he was still just a kid with big potential and bigger dreams, and among those dreams was the chance to ski with the greatest racers in the world.

A day or two before the International downhill was to be held on the Nose Dive, Molterer was at the top of the course, preparing for a fast inspection run. "It was a frightening course for the Europeans," says Kidd. "It was narrow, all ice and no fences, and after the famous first seven turns, you'd be going 75 to 80 miles an hour." Molterer, who had never raced the course before, wanted to find out just how treacherous this famously treacherous course really was. And when he took off, in his wake followed the adolescent figure of Billy Kidd.

"I managed to stay with him for the first few turns," says Kidd. "But on the seventh turn, I lost it. I slid on my chin right up to his feet." Still, for a few precious seconds, he had been able to imagine being the equal of one of the greatest racers of all time, and that, more than 40 years later, remains with Kidd as a shining memory of his youth. "It's where I got hooked on the adrenaline of racing," Kidd says.

The American International was an invention of Starr and Ruschp, the masterminds behind the development of Stowe as a world-class ski resort in the 1940s and 1950s. They figured that bringing international stars to Stowe for a ski race was as good a way as any to lift their growing resort into the limelight of international prominence. Ski racing in the 1950s was entering a golden era, riding the momentum generated by such stars as Sailer and Norway's Stein Eriksen, who along with their skiing talent brought no small amount of sex appeal to the table.

In a spur-of-the-moment decision immediately following the Olympics in Oslo, Norway, in 1952, Starr gave a call to Alice Damrosch Kiaer, manager of the U.S. Women's Team. He wanted

the Olympic medalists to compete in Stowe, he told Kiaer. The U.S. National Alpine Championships were already being held in Stowe that spring, but that wasn't enough for Starr. He wanted to embellish the event with an extra patina of international glamour.

"Just phone 'em long distance and fix it up," Starr reportedly told Kiaer. "I'll take care of the plane tickets." And so a few days later, Eriksen and Austria's Othmar Schneider, the stars of the 1952 Games, having each won a gold and silver medal, were joined in Stowe by other international racers—jet-lagged and a bit befuddled by the last-minute addition to their schedules.

Racers representing Austria, Italy, Canada, France, Japan, Norway and Switzerland came to compete—an impressively international cast given the last-minute planning. For added star value, Andrea Mead Lawrence, the suddenly famous American

who had won two gold medals in Oslo, was also in Stowe, to compete in the National Championships.

Expense was not spared. A timing system from Longines was brought in from Europe, and Stowe technicians worked overtime to refine the system even further (see page 149). Longines timers were considered the high state of the art; the 1952 Olympics marked the first in which Longines—subsequently used in all Summer and Winter Olympics—would be the official timer. The visiting racers were put up in style in the Lodge, and handsome awards were prepared. In its April newsletter after the event, the Mt. Mansfield Ski Club (MMSC) reported that "everyone agreed the trophies were the finest and most practical ever awarded for an Alpine Event."

Lured by the appeal of both the International and the

Andrea Mead Lawrence, the only American woman to win two gold medals in Olympic ski racing, was a dominant force at the 1952 National Championships.

National Championships, an estimated 8,000 to 15,000 race fans turned up. Twenty professional photographers and more than 30 journalists were there, with all the major newspapers represented. And according to local skier Gordon Manning, "more moving pictures and television film were made during the races than ever have been here before."

By all accounts, the racing in the International lived up to its billing. The young Canadian star, Ernie McCulloch, surprised the star-studded field by winning the downhill on the Nose Dive in record time. The write-up in the MMSC newsletter was effusive: "Long will we remember Ernie McCulloch's wild dash through the Seven Turns and the smooth, effortless runs of [Stein] Eriksen and Othmar Schneider." On the women's side, Andrea Mead Lawrence held up her end of the prestige-build-

ing bargain by sweeping the slalom, downhill and combined titles in the National Championships.

If a spot in the international limelight was what Starr and Ruschp were looking for in 1952, they certainly got it. This invention of theirs, the American International, through the 1950s, became an effective marketing device for spreading the Stowe gospel abroad. In European circles, ski racing was like marketing currency. Pretty much the only other resort in America to challenge Stowe's preeminence was Aspen, which also put itself on the international map through racing—by hosting the World Alpine Championships in 1950 and the renowned Roch Cup races.

But if Starr and Ruschp invented the American International, they certainly did not invent ski racing at Stowe. Almost as soon as

Dick Durrance, the first great American ski racer, competed in several important races in the late 1930s in Stowe.

the last tree on the first trail on Mt. Mansfield was cut, ski racing in Stowe began, attracting the best racers in the country.

On February 11, 1934, about three months after the Civilian Conservation Corps crews, under the guidance of Charlie Lord, went to work clearing trails, the first race was held on the Bruce, the first completed trail. That none of the participants had ever raced before wasn't surprising; downhill racing in the United States barely existed in 1934. The only recognized racecourse anywhere in the country at the time was a carriage road on Mt. Moosilauke in New Hampshire.

As a result, it might not have been the prettiest race in Stowe history. A number of years later, Alan Hadley wrote in the MMSC newsletter that "a lack of polish resulted in some mighty spills and great sitzmarks." The race was won by Jack Allen, the golf champion of Burlington, in a less-than-dazzling time of 10 minutes 48

seconds—at an average speed of under 20 miles an hour. Still, the event was enough to impress the *Burlington Free Press*, which in the next day's edition reported: "The trail proved very fast and compared favorably with the Mt. Moosilauke speedway in New Hampshire, the yardstick of downhill racing in this country."

It apparently also got the attention of Dick Durrance, the Dartmouth competitor who was beginning to build up a résumé that would mark him as the first great American ski racer. Durrance showed up two weeks later to check out the newly cut trail on Mt. Mansfield, and Charlie Lord described the performance of the young star:

"February 25, 1934, was an ideal day—clear, cool and no wind. After breakfast at Ranch Camp, we [several racers] climbed up Mansfield via the Houston Trail and the Toll Road.

Stowe's first great racer was Bob Bourdon. Even in the 1930s, he was expert at multi-tasking.

The race started at the junction of the Bruce and Toll Road…at 11:00 A.M. Dick Durrance won, being more than a minute ahead of the next runner. Later on in the village, he also won the slalom and jumping—he sure showed the local runners how to ski."

As a race trail, the Bruce might have been a fair match for the run at Mt. Moosilauke. But by the end of 1934, it was, at least for racing purposes, already on its way to obsolescence. A year later, the Nose Dive would be ready for action, to claim its position for the next four decades as one of the great race trails in the country.

The first sanctioned race on the Nose Dive—under the aegis of the U.S. Eastern Amateur Ski Association(USEASA)—was held on February 22, 1936. A young skier named Bob Bourdon of Woodstock—who would later become a regular on the Stowe skiing scene—was the winner, taking advantage of a significant edge he had over Stowe locals. For a brief couple of years, Woodstock had been the national center of lift-served skiing; the country's first rope tow had been installed in Woodstock in 1934, and other tows—including the steepest in the country at Suicide Six—were soon in operation in the area. To train and hone his technique, Bourdon could log several runs in a day by using the tows. Skiers in Stowe, where the first tow wouldn't go in until the 1936-37 season, were limited to the slow and laborious process of climbing for every run.

It was in the next winter, though, that the Nose Dive—and Stowe along with it—burst into national ski-racing prominence. Ironically, the catalyst was an event that was never supposed to happen, at least not in Stowe. The U.S. Eastern Amateur Ski Association Championships of 1937 were scheduled for the

Winter Meets Spring: The Sugar Slalom

Roland Palmedo, one of the godfathers of Stowe skiing, came up with the idea—an event to celebrate the end of the ski season and the coming of spring. In Vermont, there is no surer sign of spring's coming than the onset of maple-sugaring season. As the days gain a spring-like warmth, the maple sap begins to run, and in sugarhouses throughout the state, the process of boiling sap into syrup gets underway. And there is nothing more symbolic of the juncture of winter and spring than the tradition of sugar on snow: syrup boiled to a molasses-thick consistency and poured steaming onto the cold snow, forming a taffy-like confection.

So Palmedo conceived a late-season event that would combine racing and sugaring: The Sugar Slalom, joining winter and spring.

The first race, in 1939, was held late in the year, on April 30, after the sugaring season had pretty much run its course. But the snowfall that winter had been particularly healthy, and a good snowpack had survived well into April. The race was held on the Nose Dive, and with the coming of the first chairlift still a year away, everything—race gates, timing equipment and the precious maple syrup—had to be hauled up the mountain on toboggans.

About 40 competitors participated. Milt Hutchinson was the men's winner, and Sis McKeon the women's winner. And when the race ended, "sugar on snow was served by the Stowe-Mansfield Association, with Andy Manfield and Dwight Wilshire presiding," according to the report of the venerable Charlie Lord. So began a tradition that has reached into the present.

The Sugar Slalom was conceived initially as a "fun race," the sort of event in which prizes are given for such things as best costume. Over the years, it has evolved into a fairly serious sanctioned race, primarily for aspiring juniors. But the fun-race spirit endures, at least among the race coaches overseeing the event. "The Sugar Slalom," says local skier Kim Brown, "is when the coaches really let their hair down. They set up a bar in the sugar shack and a grill in the woods. It turns into a real carnivore's paradise." And, of course, the meaty repast and alcoholic refreshment is supplemented with sugar on snow, a Sugar Slalom tradition, well into its seventh decade, that won't die.

Thunderbolt Trail on Mt. Greylock, near North Adams, Massachusetts. But rain and warm weather forced USEASA leaders to look for an alternative site. The Nose Dive in Stowe was still relatively new and untested as a venue for a major race. But it had all the right ingredients: technical difficulty in the seven turns at the top; steepness; and the promise, particularly on the lower section, of high speeds. The switch was made, and the Stowe skiing community scrambled to prepare.

The crowds began to arrive on Friday, February 19, by train and by car, and the village of Stowe was quickly overwhelmed by the onslaught of visitors (see Chapter 2, page 65). For Sunday's downhill race, a crowd 10,000 strong (by Charlie Lord's estimate) lined the course to watch what promised to be a contest between the already famous Durrance brothers—Dick and Jack—of

Dartmouth and a visiting team from Switzerland. The spectators were not disappointed.

"The upper part down to the middle schuss was in good shape and quite fast," Lord wrote. "The lower section was soft [with] stumps showing." Pretty rough going by modern racecourse standards, but Jack Durrance, unfazed by the protruding obstacles, won the race in a time 10 seconds faster than Switzerland's Pierre Francioli. Jack's brother, Dick, finishing third.

Getting back to Stowe village after the race probably proved more difficult than getting down the stumpy course. The traffic jam that afternoon remains today the stuff of local legend. It was midnight before the road from the mountain to the town was clear.

With that race, Stowe began almost immediately to move swiftly to the forefront of American racing. Despite the traffic congestion,

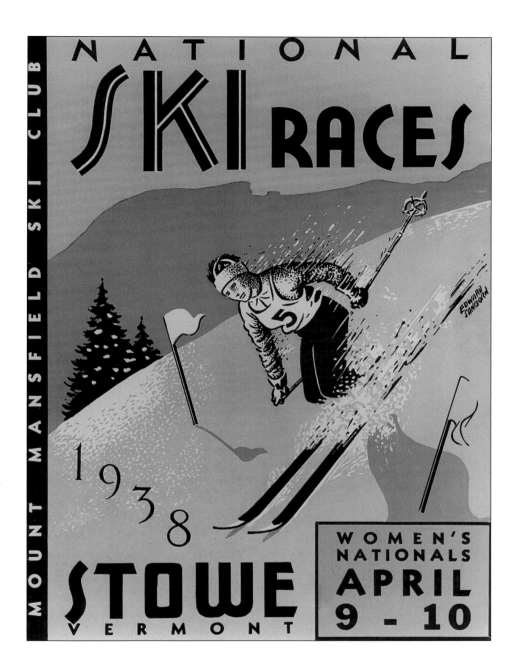

the national racing authorities were sufficiently impressed with the Nose Dive and the local ability to stage a race that they scheduled the 1938 National Championships in Stowe. It, too, proved a daunting undertaking.

Without lifts, everything necessary for the smooth running of an elite-level race, from timing equipment to rescue gear, had to be hauled by manpower up the mountain. The weather was intemperate, and the downhill, held on March 6, was run in fog, hail and rain. The next day, the second half of the slalom race had to be canceled when a blizzard descended over the mountain. As an added insult, America's great champion, Dick Durrance, was beaten in his own national championship downhill by a visiting Bavarian named Ulrich Beutter.

The local organizers came away from the event with a less-than-enthusiastic take on the proceedings. "The National races," a report in the MMSC bulletin read after the event, "were headaches and hard work for a lot of people and might as well be relegated to history."

Maybe so. But if hosting big events was all headaches and hard work, anyone involved in ski racing around Stowe would have to get used to it:1938 was just a beginning. Big events like the National and Eastern Championships would return to Stowe again and again in the coming three decades.

Stowe would welcome back the National Championships in 1952 and 1957, and host four American International events in 1952, 1955, 1957 and 1960. In 1966, Jean-Claude Killy, the glamorous Frenchman who would win three gold medals at the 1968 Olympics, led an international contingent to Stowe to compete in that era's equivalent of a World Cup race.

By 1955 the Stowe race crew was beginning to feel a little

Buddy Werner, says Billy Kidd of his teammate on the U.S. Ski Team, was "technically far ahead of his time. I wanted to ski like Buddy Werner."

more comfortable with the idea of playing big-event host. After the second International in 1955, Abner Coleman, the venerable friend of Charlie Lord who had seen Stowe skiing grow from its infancy to its major-resort status of the mid 1950s, wrote: "The second American International held so successfully last month exemplified for me the perfection that has been attained by the [Mt. Mansfield Ski Club's] race organization."

The 1955 International downhill was also noteworthy for the winner it produced in Wallace "Buddy" Werner. Werner would go on to become the best American ski racer of his era and quite possibly the best American racer ever. "Not only was he technically far ahead of everybody else," says Kidd, "he was the most competitive person I've ever seen." Werner was the rare American capable of beating the Europeans in the biggest

races—including the notorious Hahnenkamm in Kitzbühel, Austria—on their home turf. But he is probably most remembered for his misfortune—breaking his leg just before the 1960 Olympics in Squaw Valley, California, where he would have been a favorite to win gold, and dying in an avalanche shortly after finishing a disappointing eighth in the 1964 Olympic slalom.

Stowe racing history, however, can bring some of the sunnier moments in Werner's career to light. In 1955, Werner was a 19-year-old prodigy, a kid just beginning to make a name for himself in international racing circles. His world-beating efforts still lay ahead. But the 1955 International would be something of a breakthrough. Taking on some of the world's finest racers in the International, Werner blitzed the course to win in an extraordi-

Timing Is Everything

Ski racing has always depended on accurate timing—the more accurate the better. Toward that end, a number of innovative methods were developed at Stowe.

At the 1938 National Championships, surplus U.S. Army field telephones were used to time the downhill. The phones were connected by more than two miles of wire that had to be run from the start to the finish. An official at the top would telephone start times and start numbers to an official at the bottom, who could then calculate each competitor's time upon crossing the finish. Because there were sometimes as many as four racers on course at a time, and because racers often passed one another, "callers" were stationed in trees along the way, as a kind of relay system to keep the finish-line timer informed of the order of racers as they came down the mountain.

By 1952, this system—of questionable accuracy—had given way to electronic timing. The starting device sounds today like a primitive, jury-rigged toy—a piece of fiberglass fishing pole which, when pushed back by the ankles of a starting racer, would trip a refrigerator-door switch that would start the racer's running time. Yet ironically, despite the advances in technology since then, the starting devices used in modern racing aren't significantly different.

For the 1952 American International races, Sepp Ruschp decided that he wanted an electric eye at the finish to further improve timing accuracy. If Stowe was going to host world-class racers, Ruschp decided, then he wanted a timing system of similarly high caliber.

It was a daunting request. Not only had such a device not been used in American ski racing, it didn't exist. Still, Dave Partridge, the man in charge of timing and an engineer by trade, began fiddling with various electronic trinkets to come up with some sort of mechanism that would do the trick.

He experimented first with an industrial beam used for counting automobile traffic, but eventually the device that proved most effective was built from "a bag of old Navy parts" he found in his basement. A few glitches still had to be worked out on the hill, but by the time the 1952 International was ready to go in March, so was the first electronic finish-line eye to be used in American racing.

Partridge continued to refine the system over the years, but it wasn't always foolproof. In one International, as Partridge remembers, Toni Sailer, the triple gold medal winner at the 1956 Olympics, "was so happy he performed a giant geländesprung at the finish, and jumped right over the beam." The level of the beam was raised thereafter; today, it is typically set at about 18 inches above the ground.

When the professional racing circuit began making regular stops in Stowe during the 1980s, Partridge's ingenuity again came to the fore. The pro format featured head-to-head racing, and Partridge managed to rig up a system that not only calculated the time differential between two racers after each run, but also displayed it immediately on a large digital readout.

"The PA announcer went bonkers," says Partridge. "It was the first time he'd seen the results displayed like that." And that, of course, allowed him to keep attending race fans immediately informed of the progress of the race.

nary two minutes 7.5 seconds—more than nine seconds faster than the winning time recorded by Ernie McCulloch in the inaugural International three years earlier.

He would return to the International in style in 1957, arriving, as Kidd remembers, in a green Porsche he'd driven to Vermont from Colorado. The 13-year-old Kidd was impressed. "It was about then that I realized what a cool sport ski racing was," Kidd says.

Werner was back in Stowe again—without the Porsche this time—for the 1959 Vermont Alpine championships, an event that will probably find its place in history less for what happened than for its roster of participants. Scanning the results produces a who's-who of famous American racers: Werner, Tom Corcoran, Max Marolt, Jimmie Heuga, Marvin

Moriarty, Brooks Dodge, Chuck Ferries, Betsy Snite, Penny Pitou—all Olympians who happened to show up for a state championship race. As confirmation of his brilliance, Werner won the giant slalom against such an elite field by a margin of 4.5 seconds over his nearest competitor, despite falling four gates into the race.

The number of major races held in Stowe dwindled through the 1970s, but a bit of international flair would still touch the race scene. In 1980, when the Olympics were to be held in Lake Placid in the Adirondacks of New York, a number of European racers came to Stowe to train before the Games. Among the visiting delegations was the powerful Austrian team. The Austrian head coach, Karl Kahr, had already made a controversial decision by leaving the defending Olympic

Opposite: Flanking teammate Joan Hannah, American stars Penny Pitou (right) and Betsy Snite (left) won medals at the Olympics in Squaw Valley before coming to the 1960 American International in Stowe. Right: The 1960 American International attracted many Olympic medalists, both men and women. A highlight on the men's side: Guy Perillat, the Olympic downhill bronze medalist, eclipsed fellow Frenchman and gold medalist Jean Vuarnet in record time in the Nose Dive downhill.

downhill champion, Franz Klammer, off the team. Now, by taking his team from the hallowed Alps of Austria to train in foreign America, he was further risking the wrath of the Austrian public.

The Austrians figured that in Stowe they would encounter the kind of snow and climate they were likely to encounter in Lake Placid. Indeed, as Billy Kidd says, "The snow was often icy, particularly in the days before snowmaking. I loved it. It was perfect training for the Olympics." Apparently the Europeans agreed, even though by 1980 considerable snowmaking was in place on both Mt. Mansfield and Spruce Peak. Still, the cold weather, the steep terrain and the hard snow were a good match for the Olympic conditions in Lake Placid, and the decision to come to Stowe apparently paid off for the

Austrians. Leonhard Stock would be the surprise winner of the downhill, and teammate Peter Wirnsberger would finish second. Kahr must have breathed a sigh of vindicated relief.

The big events—the American International, the National Championship and others—might stand as mile markers in Stowe racing history. But they are really only small vignettes in the much larger story of Stowe racing. Racing, both past and present, cuts a wide swath through the life and culture of Stowe skiing. It is a story as much or more about the great racers who came from Stowe as it is about those, like Werner, who came to Stowe for major events. And racing runs deeper even than that, for it remains today, as it has always been, a grassroots and family affair, a part of the common language of Stowe life.

Left: Marilyn Shaw was Stowe's first great woman racer. Her one chance for Olympic glory was thwarted when the 1940 Games were cancelled due to war. Opposite: Jean-Claude Killy brought his revolutionary "jet-turn" technique to Stowe in the mid-1960s.

One of the first great champions to rise out of the Stowe fold was Marilyn Shaw, whose story, according to a *Collier's* magazine story on March 1, 1941, was "the story of a whole family of Shaws and of the town of Stowe, Vermont, too." Indeed. Her father was proprietor of the town general store, a store still in the Shaw family and still bearing the name. Her first ski teacher was her mother—Vermont's Snow Queen of 1935 and an occasional skiing partner of radio broadcaster Lowell Thomas—who would take Marilyn and her sisters up to the Toll Road in the early 1930s. Mother and children would struggle awkwardly back down the road, with little knowledge of proper technique.

When Sepp Ruschp arrived in 1936 to set up his ski school, he immediately recognized the talents of the young Marilyn and took her under his tutelage. When the National Championships came to Stowe in 1938, Marilyn was 13 years old and had never skied the infamous Nose Dive. Undeterred, she entered the race; backing away from a challenge has never been a part of the ethos of Stowe racing.

It was snowing heavily on the day of the race. "All I saw were trees and snow and I fell and fell," Marilyn told *Collier's*. Still, she managed to finish 12th among 27 starters—not bad for a 13-year-old in her first National Championships. She would go on to be named to the 1940 Olympic team—an honorary position, as it turned out, when the Olympics were canceled due to the onset of war. She did, however, manage to bring a small bit of national attention to herself in 1941 by filling in for Sonja Henie, the famous Olympic figure skater, in skiing scenes in

the movie *Sun Valley Serenade*. While Marilyn's role was small, the movie would go on to become a popular success.

The themes within Marilyn Shaw's story would repeat themselves in the ensuing decades of Stowe racing: a prodigious young talent, a family with local roots, difficult terrain and snow conditions, expert coaching, and a determination to take on any challenge that might or might not lead to an Olympic-team berth. A number of years later, another member of the family, Tiger Shaw, would become a member of the 1988 team. And not long after retiring from racing, Tiger was doing what Marilyn's mother had done almost 70 years earlier—taking his kids to the mountain to train and race.

Billy Kidd and Peter Ruschp, Sepp's son, were also raised in a culture of ski racing passed on from one generation to the next.

Sepp Ruschp, of course, had been a champion racer in Austria before coming to Stowe, and Kidd's father had been a ski jumper in Northfield, about 25 miles southeast of Stowe.

The two young racers grew up together in the 1950s, literally skiing in their own backyards. Kidd remembers that, at a very young age, he would create a makeshift ski slope behind the Buccaneer Motel, the inn his family owned on the Mountain Road. Peter grew up in the Toll House before his parents moved to town when he was three. As kids after school, "we'd climb up the Toll House and run gates until dark," says Ruschp. "For us it was like kids in the city going to the park. The Toll House slope was our park."

Stowe might have been growing rapidly as a major international ski resort at that time, but it remained, at its core, a tightly

Below: Billy Kidd (left) and Tiger Shaw (right) are two of the more than 20
Stowe skiers and snowboarders to have been named to the U.S. national team.
Opposite: Racers during pre-race inspection for a slalom in the 1950s.

knit, small-town community. "Everyone knew everyone back then," says Ruschp. "We were all part of a family." And deeply integrated into that family life was ski racing. If, by analogy, basketball was a city kid's game, then ski racing was the sport for kids growing up in a mountain town like Stowe.

Pretty soon Kidd and Ruschp would graduate to bigger and better stuff, winning ski races throughout New England and earning local acclaim as potential inheritors of the legacy left by previous famous Stowe racers. It was a legacy passed on, like a baton, from one generation to the next. Kidd remembers that his local hero growing up was Marvin Moriarty, a member of the 1956 U.S. Olympic Team. "I grew up following Marvin Moriarty and hearing stories about ski racing around

the world," says Kidd. "He was so colorful—he made ski racing seem like the most fun sport on the planet."

As a teenager, Kidd was heralded by the local race community as the person to fill Moriarty's boots. After Kidd won the 1963 Stowe Cup slalom by almost six seconds and the downhill by two seconds, the Mt. Mansfield Ski Club newsletter gushed: "It is our opinion that Billy Kidd is the racer to watch in the East...and is an outstanding prospect for an Olympic team berth in 1964."

As it turned out, of course, that assessment fell a bit short of the mark. Not only did Kidd make the 1964 Olympic team, he won a silver medal in slalom, becoming the first American man to win an Olympic medal in skiing. Peter Ruschp, earning a 10-year stint on the U.S. Ski Team, wasn't far behind.

As Kidd's career would continue to spiral upward through the

FINISH

In 1942, the so-called "Stone Hut Gang" came up with the idea of the Merry Go Round—four races on four of Stowe's most challenging trails in one weekend.

1960s, culminating with a gold medal in the combined in the 1970 World Championships, the next generation of Stowe racers was beginning to gets its initiation in running gates. That's just the way it is in Stowe: the racing baton passing from one generation to the next. In the 1970s, six Stowe racers made the U.S. Ski Team, followed by the likes of Tiger Shaw in the 1980s and 1990s.

This is the obvious way to document Stowe ski racing—by talking about the elite racers who've spent time here. At last count, more than 20 Stowe skiers (and more recently, snowboarders) have been members of the national team. But a complete picture of Stowe racing through the years also requires more than a passing glance at the grassroots culture that produced so many top competitors and endures robustly in the present.

"There has always been a race culture here, going back to the 1930s," says Kim Brown, who in his 50s continues to compete in

Stowe's weekly ski-bum races. "Racing began here, and racers were our heroes. Guys like Bob Bourdon, our first great ski racer—that was the kind of guy we all wanted to be like."

Brown is right, of course. Almost as soon as Stowe's first trail—the Bruce—was cut in 1934, racing began. But it certainly wasn't all about making national or Olympic teams. Stowe's racing tradition has always been less rooted in the hopes of a select few who might reach the elite ranks of the sport than in a widely felt desire to compete just for the pure and simple thrill of competing. In Stowe, racing is not an elitist sport; it is the sport of everyman. Those first racers in 1934 didn't dream of Olympic achievement; Alpine ski racing, after all, wouldn't be added to the Olympic roster until two years later. They did it because they figured a little competition made the skiing more interesting.

That mindset was certainly prevalent in the Merry Go Round,

From Club Skier to Olympian: One Stowe Skier's Story

Erik Schlopy had already shown some promise as an 11-year-old ski racer when he moved with his family from Buffalo, New York, to Stowe in the mid 1980s. But his talent was still relatively raw and undeveloped; in size alone, the small hills of western New York had obvious limitations. Stowe, on the other hand, was, as Schlopy says, "the big leagues. It was a big mountain, and Vermont was such a hotbed for high-caliber racing." He entered the Mt. Mansfield Ski Club (MMSC) program under the guidance of Mark Hutchinson, a coach who taught him "how to ski the whole mountain, all this different terrain." Three days a week, Schlopy and other racers would leave the local junior high school early in the afternoon for on-course training or free skiing on trails like the Goat, Starr and National. "Hutch really knew how to nurture the spirit of skiing," says Schlopy. "For him, it was all about putting smiles on kids' faces." Apparently it worked. Schlopy made what he calls "a huge jump" in the two full years he spent in the MMSC program. "In the year I was 13," he says, "I won 26 of 28 races. And in the two races I didn't win, I fell." He was on his way. After junior high

in Stowe, Schlopy attended nearby Burke Mountain Academy, one of the country's leading schools for ski racers, and from there, the rest is history. He has since gone on to garner several U.S. National Alpine Championships and a spot on two U.S. Olympic teams. In 2001, Schlopy was the best giant slalom skier in the United States, ranking third in the world.

There were several stops along the way in his career path—Buffalo, Stowe, Burke Mountain, the U.S. Ski Team, a professional-racing stint and back to the Ski Team. Still, Schlopy regards his years with the Mt. Mansfield Ski Club as pivotal. "Without the move to Stowe, I wouldn't have become a two-time Olympian," he says. Much of that, of course, had to do with the development of his skiing skills, but it went beyond that. The move to Stowe was, for Schlopy, a "mental breakthrough," jump-starting a new self-confidence in discovering that he had the ability to compete, and win, in the big leagues. And it nurtured something deeper still, more lasting even than ski racing success. "The love of the sport," says Schlopy. "That's what I got from that program."

a race conceived in 1942 by the Stone Hut Gang, a group that often encamped in the Stone Hut below the Nose in order to be ready in the morning for a fresh start of downhill skiing. The idea behind the Merry Go Round was to run a series of races over a weekend on four of Stowe's most challenging trails at the time: Nose Dive, Steeple, Bruce and Chin Clip.

It would be a legitimate athletic challenge, of course, and many of the competitors would certainly be out to win. But as Robert Fletcher—the so-called "scribe of the Stone Hut Gang"—described the race, "50 to 60 percent…were purely recreational skiers… But they had asked for a downhill to end all downhills, and this was it… They ran all the way from weekend beavers to experts and everything in between. The atmosphere was informal, and even the officials were out to enjoy themselves for once."

A similar spirit endures today in the regular Tuesday ski-bum races, which have been held since the early 1970s. Weekly ski-bum races are common at other resorts, of course, but at Stowe they have become an entrenched and bristlingly active institution. On an average Tuesday, between 35 and 45 four-person teams show up—as many as 180 weekend beavers, experts and everything in between. Few come with illusions of posting the fastest time, although a complicated handicapping system helps level the playing field. Instead, they come, as Brown says, "just to be involved, just to enjoy the whole opportunity to race. It's a great scene, a great party."

The tentacles of Stowe's racing culture reach in other directions as well. The roots of the ski school reach into the European racing tradition, founded by Sepp Ruschp, himself a champion, and built around such instructors as Othmar Schneider. After

Opposite: Billy Woods, killed in a car crash as a teenager, "had enough talent to beat the world," says Billy Kidd. "He was one of the few people who could beat Buddy Werner." Right: Suzy Chaffee. Below: Mt. Mansfield Ski Club members gather before a race in the 1970s.

winning his Olympic medals and competing in the first International in 1952, Schneider joined forces in the Stowe ski school with Ruschp. Even the *Stowe Reporter*, the town's weekly newspaper, was "almost built on ski racing," says the paper's publisher, Biddle Duke. For years, the paper's front-page story, as often as not, has had something to do with ski racing, although the paper has broadened its news coverage in recent years. "We still take our ski-racing heritage very seriously," says Duke.

So does the Mt. Mansfield Ski Club, which not only runs the ski-bum races and other events but also oversees Stowe's youth-development program with more than 200 junior racers, snowboarders, and freestyle competitors. The program, says the club's executive director, Tom Sequist, continues to grow, "enduring through the years" despite all the other things—like youth hockey

and the town's new swimming pool—that might draw kids away.

"We've got very deep roots," Sequist goes on, "and there's a chain link. Kids are definitely influenced by the athletes who've come before them who've gone on to the [U.S.] ski team." The most recent athletes to emulate are Erik Schlopy and Chip Knight, both 2002 Olympians who went through the youth program at Stowe.

Still, for every Olympian in the making there are hundreds of racers in Stowe, both kids and adults, who compete just for the hell of it. That's the real legacy of Stowe racing—the grassroots passion for competition that lives today in events like the ski-bum races and the season-ending Sugar Slalom, bonding through the generations to the spirit of those first racers who climbed the Bruce Trail in 1934. ▨

The popularity of ski touring—above on Bull Moose Hill—in
the 1930s faded with the arrival of downhill skiing.

CHAPTER 7

Birth and Rebirth: Cross-Country Skiing

It is a damp and gray afternoon in late January, in the midst of the thaw that arrives in Vermont at about the same time every year with the predictability of an incoming tide. The skiing conditions are less than ideal; the snow is a soft, warm mash and the going laborious.

Even so, about three dozen cross-country skiers have assembled at the Topnotch Nordic Barn for a four-kilometer time-trial race, part of a Wednesday-afternoon race series held throughout the winter in Stowe. The weather and snow conditions might be imperfect, but the competitive enthusiasm is palpable. There are racers of all ages and abilities, from 10-year-old girls in loose-fitting snow pants to a Lycra-clad team of sponsored athletes to men over 60 in enviably fit condition. The token star of this afternoon's affair—Stowe has a way of attracting ultra-jocks whenever the whiff of competition is in the air—is the affable Mark Gilbertson, a 1998 Olympian.

In the warmth of the Barn, with its polished, wide-planked floor and pine beams overhead, the competitors sign up and collect their race bibs at a desk beneath a large west-facing window. A cloud-shrouded Mt. Mansfield rises in the background, appearing as a tessellated mural through the window's 8-by-10-inch panes. In the foreground, the meadows of Topnotch will serve as the competition venue.

Once the racing begins, it is clear that no one will beat Gilbertson or come even close; he finishes a minute and a half ahead of the next fastest competitor. Bringing up the rear are the 10-year-olds, their hats sliding down across their foreheads and over their eyes, as they slog home in the enveloping darkness of the coming evening.

This hardcore group, young and old and equally oblivious to the inclement elements, represents the soul of a cross-country culture with deep roots in the Stowe community. Cross-country skiing might not have been born in Stowe, but in Stowe it was given a new life that sustains the sport today, both locally and around the country.

Cross-country skiing (using the term, very liberally, to refer to anything other than downhill skiing) arrived early in Stowe—well before downhill skiing. Exactly when the first skis were put to snow, or by whom, is not a matter of historical record, although it's not unlikely that someone was using something that might loosely be called skis before the onset of the 20th century.

After all, skiing and ski jumping were sporadically practiced in other parts of the country in the mid to late 1800s. Miners in the Sierra Nevada mountains of California, mostly of Scandinavian descent, held cross-country races in the 1850s. It gave them some-

Opposite: Charlie Lord, the man who laid out the first trail network on Mt. Mansfield, was also an accomplished cross-country skier. Right: After cross-country skiing experienced a renaissance in Stowe in the 1970s, snowshoeing gained popularity in the 1990s.

thing to bet on—a 19th-century miner's version of horse racing or prize fighting. Also in the 1850s, a legendary Norwegian nicknamed Snowshoe Thompson traveled on skis through deep snows to deliver mail to remote locations in the Sierra. In 1887, the first ski-jumping competition in the country was held in Red Wing, Minnesota.

So it is possible that someone in Stowe, on barrel staves or some other makeshift device, tried skiing at about the same time. Yet there is no documented account of skiing in Stowe until 1902, when Craig Burt and some fellow lumbermen tried sliding down small hills on handmade skis. It was a short-lived experiment. Burt and friends quickly dismissed their efforts as not particularly enjoyable (see page 33), and within a few years pretty much gave up on skiing altogether.

Still, cross-country skiing, as Thompson had amply demonstrated in California, could have a utilitarian purpose that wasn't necessarily about the recreational enjoyment that Burt had apparently been seeking. In winter environments in an era predating the wide use of the automobile, skis represented an effective mode of cross-country transportation. That was something that Scandinavian families who migrated to Stowe in the early part of the 20th century understood well.

According to the written recollections of Charlie Lord, "around 1912, and on for several years, there were three Scandinavian families located in Stowe—one on West Hill, one on Edson Hill and the other on Shaw Hill… They traveled back and forth on cross-country skis. They couldn't speak much English, but they knew how to ski."

A vast trail network—more than 100 miles of groomed trails as well as backcountry trails—make escape into the backcountry easy.

Craig Burt described the Scandinavians as "utility skiers on utility skis." But he might have been unduly dismissive in characterizing the skis as not much more than utilitarian tools. According to Carrie Slayton, a resident of nearby Moscow at the time, the skis were made with a craftsman's sensibilities. Writing many years later, Slayton gave the following account of the efforts of Lars Svedin, patriarch of one of the Scandinavian families, to make skis for his family: "He went to Mr. Fred Smith for lumber, and he chose good old rock maple. This was then planed and ripped at Smith's parcel-handling factory. In his shop at home, under his own handicraft and with the aid of two older girls, he drawshaved, shaped, steam-curved and painted the finished skis, which were a work of art in themselves. He made two types—a long, slim, very slender ski for cross-country and a wider one with grooves for jumping."

The Scandinavians' unusual activity did not go without notice. Other Stowe residents quickly became intrigued by the idea of skiing not just for transportation but as sport. Along with tobogganing and snowshoeing, it was something to keep school-children entertained outdoors in winter. For a brief period, Svedin apparently developed a small cottage industry as a ski maker. Henry McMahon, whose father worked in Smith's factory, recalled years later how Svedin made him a pair of skis for the winter of 1913-14: "I was 11 years old. Father bought them for me—just skis, no poles. I had to make those. I believe he paid one dollar and a half for [the skis]… They were rock maple, no grooves on the bottom, and the harnesses [bindings] were made of belting from Smith's mill, mortised into sides with rawhide lacing over the top of the toe for adjustment."

The Catamount Trail

The idea of a 300-mile cross-country ski route through Vermont, from the Massachusetts border to the Canadian border, had a curious beginning. It was not the product of some great cooperative effort in master planning. Instead, it was one guy's dream project. Steven Bushey, a University of Vermont graduate student in geography, decided to do his thesis on a theoretical trans-Vermont winter route. The project involved not just mapping but also obtaining easements for passage across both public and private land.

That was the Catamount Trail in theory; when Bushey and his friends Paul Jarris and Ben Rose actually skied the route—or something approximating today's route—the Catamount Trail became a reality. Or at least it opened the door to reality. For what lay ahead was plenty of trail maintenance and improvement, along with the on-going process of securing rights of way. It remains today a work in progress.

Still, by the turn of the millennium, Bushey's original vision had more or less been fulfilled—a state-long route connecting backcountry trails with informal routes across private property and groomed trails at Nordic centers. As such, it is the longest cross-country ski trail in the country, making possible the kind of multiday, inn-to-inn tour that is popular in Scandinavia but all but unheard of in the United States.

Of course, few skiers attempt to ski the entire 300 miles in one trip. A day trip, an overnight trip—that's the way most people go. Toward that end, the trail is now broken down into 26 separate tours, a convenient number for alphabetization from A to Z, south to north. Each tour is manageable in a day of skiing.

One of the most scenic sections of the trail passes through the heart of Stowe cross-country-skiing territory. Tour S runs from Bolton to the Trapp Family Lodge (see page 172), and section T extends from the Trapp Family Lodge to Edson Hill Manor, with the Bolton–Trapp's route an exemplar of Vermont back-country skiing.

The route runs 12 miles from Bolton into the Nebraska Valley before joining with the Trapp's trail network. It drops 2,000 vertical feet through the predominately maple and birch forests on the northeast facade of Bolton Mountain. It is a trail that demands a full quiver of backcountry skills—touring skills, the ability to make precise turns in close, wooded quarters, the ability to deal with snow conditions varying from powder to solid ice and route-finding. It is this combination of elements—along, of course, with the inherent natural beauty of the trail—that makes it "the most renowned tour in the state of Vermont," according to Trapp's Charlie Yerrick.

If McMahon was like other kids of the time, he used his new skis both for play and as a means of getting around. According to Slayton's account, a number of Stowe-area children used skis to get to school and back, and that was certainly not the only transportational use of skis. As Slayton recalled: "All who skied in those days could go anywhere they wanted to go on skis, as there was no sand, salt and little traffic on the roads."

A few hardy young men were more adventurous. Through the 1910s and 1920s, ski tours through the meadows and hillsides around Mansfield were common. A typical tour might involve a visit to a logging camp, where the participants might sit around an open fire, drink hot chocolate and roast apples. When ambitions were especially high, someone might organize a tour through Smugglers' Notch to Jeffersonville. In 1925, for example,

Stowe School skiers journeyed through the Notch to participate in the Jeffersonville Winter Carnival. It was an all-male outing. The girls, in what presumably was considered a safer and more womanly means of transport, were shuttled to and from Jeffersonville by car.

Perhaps nothing did more to spark interest in Nordic skiing than the first Stowe Winter Carnival held in 1921. The carnival put the spectacle of ski jumping front and center; competitors soared off a jump, built near the town of Stowe, that by the standard of the day was enormous. An appreciative audience was apparently hooked. Pretty soon, home-built jumps were appearing in backyards throughout the Stowe area, with a number of more professionally constructed jumps built on hills from Waterbury to Stowe for serious competitions and exhibitions.

This was in keeping with a boom in interest in ski jumping around the country during the first quarter of the century. In the 1910s and 1920s, downhill skiing had yet to take off as a sport in the United States, and cross-country skiing was practiced primarily by a handful of die-hard adherents, mostly of Scandinavian descent. For either downhill or cross-country skiing, there was little in the way of competition.

Ski jumping, on the other hand, had entered its heyday in America. Ski-jumping competitions became the central spectacle of winter carnivals, in Stowe as elsewhere around the country. After the demonstrated popularity of ski jumping in the 1911 Dartmouth Winter Carnival in Hanover, New Hampshire—the first winter carnival to be held in the United States—jumping competitions were

regularly held almost anywhere in the country where there were hills and snow.

The real skiing heroes of the era—people like Alf Engen, who would go on later to found Alta ski area in Utah—were jumpers. The only skiing competition at the first Winter Olympics, held in 1924 in Chamonix, France, was in jumping. In that Olympics, American Anders Haugen was the bronze medalist—the first and still only American to win a ski-jumping medal.

Cross-country skiing competition was a little slower to catch on. But cross-country races were a part of the second Stowe Winter Carnival—still well before downhill races were even contemplated—and remained a part of the action, in one form or another, for the duration of the carnival's history.

But interest in both jumping and cross-country skiing began

Below: *After the popularity of the first Stowe Winter Carnival in 1921,*
a number of ski jumps were built in the Stowe and Waterbury area.
Opposite: Ski touring from the Summit House below the Nose on Mt. Mansfield.

to wane in the late 1920s and early 1930s, and ironically it was another form of skiing that caused the downturn. By the late 1920s, word began filtering in from Europe, brought back by world travelers like Roland Palmedo, of the new sport of downhill skiing catching on fast in the Alps.

For the average person, jumping was athletically too difficult and potentially dangerous. Cross-country skiing required more effort than the average person was willing to expend. And perhaps downhill skiing, too, would have languished as the sport of a dedicated few. But the arrival of tows and lifts in the 1930s did away with the toil of hiking uphill, and downhill skiing as a sport with broad popular appeal was on its way.

The enthusiasm of people like Palmedo and Stowe downhill pioneers such as Charlie Lord and Abner Coleman might have sparked an initial interest in downhill skiing. But there is little doubt that the development of mechanical uphill transportation put a torch to the fire. David Rowan, publisher of Ski Area Management magazine, explained the rapid rise of downhill skiing in simplest terms: "Not having to climb triggered the growth." By 1940, with several tows and lifts in place in Stowe and elsewhere, downhill skiing was said to have more than a million adherents around the country. Nordic skiing was more or less steamrolled by downhill skiing's rapid rise in popularity. And the onset of World War II didn't help matters.

Cross-country skiing did get a reinvigorating lift toward the end of the war years when Sepp Ruschp and Erling Strom (see page 177), two great men of the mountains, concocted the idea of the Stowe Derby. According to widely accepted lore, the genesis

of the Derby goes something like this:

On a fall day in 1944, Strom and Ruschp were on Mt. Mansfield clearing brush from ski trails. Perhaps to divert his attention from the hard labor at hand, Strom idly proposed to Ruschp a challenge. Cross-country skiers, he suggested, were better all-round skiers than their downhill counterparts. A race from the top of Mt. Mansfield to the village of Stowe, requiring both downhill and cross-country skills, would prove it.

One can envision Ruschp, sweating and covered in sawdust, bark and twigs, contemplating the proposition and evaluating his chances. As a former cross-country champion himself, he presumed himself to be a reasonable adversary for the Norwegian, even if downhill skiing was his forte. The challenge was accepted; the race was born.

There are variations on this story, as there always are when history turns hazy with the passage of time. Strom in his autobiography wrote that the real germ of the idea for the Derby grew out of discussions he had with another Norwegian cross-country enthusiast, Rolf Holtvedt, because "we hated to see our favorite type of skiing neglected." But there's probably some truth in both versions, for Ruschp was very much a part of the organization of that first Derby. And when it was held, on February 28, 1945, he settled the mythical score with Strom by winning the race.

Ruschp covered the 10-mile course—roughly four miles down the Toll Road and then six miles into the village of Stowe—in a time of one hour and three minutes. That was good enough to beat Strom by two minutes, although the 46-year-old Strom could point to the fact that he had spotted the junior Ruschp 10 years in

age. Ten other competitors participated in that first race.

Despite Strom's and Ruschp's passionate interest in the Derby, however, the race was never able to attract more than 27 competitors in its first eight years. Cross-country skiing in the 1950s simply couldn't compete for the public's attention with the fast-growing sport of downhill skiing. In 1954, with interest and participation flagging, the Derby came to an end.

Or at least seemingly so. For in 1972, rising from a renewed surge in interest in cross-country skiing in Stowe, the Derby discovered new life. In its new incarnation, it would go on to become what it is today: part race, part pageant, part spectacle and part crash-fest, with many competitors going down hard in trying to negotiate the icy Toll Road on cross-country skis.

The Derby now attracts more than 500 competitors annually, for what one 2002 competitor called "just crazy fun." It is one of the highlights of the Stowe winter, everything that Ruschp and Strom must originally have envisioned on a mountain trail in the fall of 1944. But if the Derby can trace its roots to Strom and Ruschp, it must also give indirect credit for its revitalization in no small part to the vision and efforts of a famous family named von Trapp.

The von Trapp family story is of course a part of American lore. It is the story of *The Sound of Music*: A musically gifted family living in the scenic Tyrol leaves behind its home and worldly possessions, escaping the clutches of Naziism to emigrate to America. In the Trapp Family Lodge between Stowe and Moscow, photos and posters hang conspicuously on the lodge walls, documenting the family's history and musical successes.

The von Trapp family contribution to the revival of cross-country skiing in America might seem to be not much more than an incidental footnote in the family's legendary tale of heroism, stoicism and redemption. But within the culture of cross-country skiing, the decision by Johannes von Trapp, president of the Lodge, to create a touring center in 1968 is a seminal milestone.

At around that time, cross-country skiing and touring was experiencing a modest resurgence of interest in America, in part as a reaction against what many perceived as an overdevelopment and commercialization of downhill skiing. Cross-country skiing fit neatly with the "back to nature" movement that was part of the '60s-era ethos. But cross-country skiers in the 1960s went mostly about their business in a casual and impromptu way. The operative concept: head for the woods and tromp around on skis for a while.

Among those who picked up an interest in cross-country skiing in the 1960s was Johannes von Trapp. He had competed as a cross-country skier in college and, during winter breaks from college, would come back to the family lodge with a Norwegian roommate to ski around on old logging roads and trails. "I figured that if we were having so much fun, then guests [at the lodge] would probably enjoy it, too," says Johannes. So a few years later, he began putting the pieces together of what would become the first commercial cross-country ski center in America.

The family had begun welcoming summer guests as early as the late 1940s, largely as a way of filling empty rooms at the farm while the family was performing on tour around the country. Given the size of the family—10 siblings strong—there were

plenty of rooms to fill. As summer business flourished and demand increased, the original farmhouse was expanded into a lodge.

Winter business, on the other hand, was relatively meager. Johannes figured that something unique—something other than downhill skiing at nearby Mt. Mansfield—was needed to attract guests to the lodge in winter. That something, he decided in the fall of 1967, was cross-country skiing. It made good sense: With hundreds of acres of rolling hillsides in a bucolic mountain environment and with a reliable snowpack, the lodge was ideally situated for the creation of a touring center.

What Johannes needed, however, was a person of similar vision and enthusiasm to run the show. Toward that end, he circulated an advertisement, for a skiing director, in Norway. Close to 300 applicants responded to the ad, but Johannes never got

beyond the first interview. Per Sorlie was so obviously the man for the job—handsome, personable, skilled as a skier and trained in hotel management. Johannes hired him immediately without interviewing any other candidates, and he never looked back.

"Per was a success from the beginning," he says. "He was very popular with our clientele. The success of the program I attribute largely to his energy and his charm in those early years." There was nothing outwardly fancy about the operation in those early years; the "touring center" operated out of a garage at the lodge. The rental skis were wooden klunkers. But Sorlie embellished the program with the classic panache of a European guide or instructor. He would ingratiate himself among guests and become, for the duration of their stay, virtually a member of their extended family. Whatever the original touring center might have lacked in

Opposite: The Trapp Family Lodge, rebuilt in 1983 after a fire, was the focal point of a cross-country skiing revival in the U.S. in the late 1960s. The famous von Trapp family first came to Stowe in 1939.

physical structure was more than compensated for by Sorlie's character, energy and style.

As Charlie Yerrick, head of the Trapp Family Lodge Tour Center, says, "Per was quite a socially energetic personality at dinner at night." He would join lodge guests at the dinner table and entertain them with stories of skiing, and in short order sell them on the idea of joining him or one of his fellow Norwegian instructors on a cross-country skiing tour the following day. Larry Damon, a member of four U.S. Olympic cross-country teams who was instrumental in some of the early trail-grooming efforts at the lodge, says, "Those first Norwegian instructors lived in the lodge and were part of the nightly entertainment."

In those first couple of years, says Yerrick, "this was a touring center, not a cross-country skiing center." In saying so, Yerrick is

making a distinction between the type of relatively fast-paced aerobic skiing, on groomed tracks, that is popular today as opposed to the kind of extended, guided tours that were the focus at the lodge in the early years. In an interesting twist of historical coincidence, some of the best touring routes led into and around the Ranch Valley, the birthplace (at Ranch Camp) of downhill skiing on Mt. Mansfield in the mid 1930s.

Within a few short years, it became clear that Johannes von Trapp had hit upon an idea that was right for its time. "It was all quite successful from the start," says von Trapp. "Our business doubled after the first year and continued to double in each of the first few years. Our winter business hadn't been very good, and cross-country skiing turned that around."

But what was happening at the Trapp Family Lodge wasn't an

isolated phenomenon. As Yerrick says, "Cross-country skiing in the '70s was booming." In fact, the boom was pronounced enough for others in the Stowe area to follow Johannes' lead. Nearby Edson Hill Manor opened a touring center in the early 1970s, and Stowe Mountain Resort would soon do the same, with a trail network adjacent to (and connecting with) the Trapp Family Lodge terrain. Topnotch Resort and Spa entered the fold as well, with trails running primarily through the meadows along the valley floor between Stowe village and Mt. Mansfield.

Von Trapp's concept—the cross-country ski resort—would also spread quickly well beyond Stowe. The development of downhill ski resorts, after a boom period in the 1960s with the creation of such resorts as Vail, Snowbird and Jackson Hole, entered almost complete dormancy by the late 1970s. At the same time, smaller, local downhill ski areas began disappearing at a rapid rate.

But following the Trapp Family Lodge lead, cross-country centers began cropping up all across the country in the 1970s. In addition to large resorts like Royal Gorge, in California, and the Jackson Touring Center, in New Hampshire, hundreds of smaller areas entered the cross-country fold. Many of the smaller areas came and went quickly. Still, the Vermont Ski Areas Association today lists 30 cross-country centers in Vermont alone—almost double the number of downhill areas listed by the association, and a roster that is certainly not a complete representation of the state's cross-country opportunities.

Very quickly, then, the basic elements of a substantial cross-country skiing destination were in place in Stowe, where you

Erling Strom, Mountain Master

Erling Strom was a man's man. He lived in Stowe for 30 years, running a lodge that bore his name and promoting his great love, cross-country skiing, in whatever way he could. The first Stowe Derby, held in 1945, was principally Strom's idea. But in the realm of adventure, Erling Strom was well-known before he made a name for himself in Stowe.

By the time Strom arrived in Stowe in 1940 at the age of 42, his accomplishments were groundbreaking and legendary. Born in Norway in 1898, Strom in his early 20s moved to Arizona, where he learned, among other things, to pick up rattlesnakes with his bare hands without being bitten. But Arizona was probably not the right place for someone so devoted to winter sports. So he moved Fort Collins, Colorado, where he found work as an oilfield roustabout. While there, his attentions turned to ski jumping in nearby Estes Park, and he became an accomplished enough jumper to win the U.S. Combined Jumping and Cross-Country Skiing Championships.

A few years later he was hired as a ski instructor in Lake Placid, New York—a rare and pioneering

profession at that time. But he also became transfixed with the big mountains of British Columbia and Alaska. In 1931, he assembled and led a party that would become the first to reach the Snow Dome at the center of the enormous Columbia Icefields in the Canadian Rockies in winter. The 255-mile round trip on skis took 16 days. A year later, with his climbing partner Al Lindley, Strom would lead a party on the first ascent of both the north and south summits of Mt. McKinley in Alaska. It was a feat that certified his mountaineering fame.

Strom's legacy lives on in the Canadian Rockies, where he was instrumental in building backcountry lodges, still used today, in the Skoki Valley and at the foot of Mt. Assiniboine, the so-called "Matterhorn of the Rockies." The Strom legacy in Stowe is dimmer, now that the Strom lodge is long gone. Still, the world-traveling mountain man developed a particular fondness for Stowe, and he and his wife opened their lodge in the 1940s. "We fell for the charming little town and its beautiful surroundings," he wrote in his 1977 autobiography, "not to mention its skiing possibilities."

could come for a week of cross-country skiing and never ski the same tour twice. It was a concept unprecedented in the United States. What remained was for the four contiguous ski centers to refine, improve and expand upon what they had.

One obvious area for improvement was trail grooming. Because there was really no such thing as mechanical trail grooming in the United States at the time, the first groomers had more or less to make things up as they went along. Larry Damon remembers one of the first machines used at the Trapp Family Lodge, a modified snowmobile called a "mogul planer" with a blade dragged over the snow to create a somewhat smoother skiing surface. It was far from perfect, but it made for much easier skiing than slogging

through deep, unpacked snow or on trails that had been packed by guides or instructors on skis. And it was just a beginning, for it wouldn't be long before more sophisticated machines were brought with special devices to set neat, uniform ski tracks.

When Bill Koch, the first and only American male to win an Olympic cross-country medal (a silver in the 30-kilometer race in 1976), popularized skate skiing in the mid 1970s, the Stowe ski centers were quick to make smooth, open tracks for skating a part of their grooming repertoire.

There's no doubt that advances in grooming spurred the growth of a more aerobic form of cross-country skiing compared with slower-paced, long-distance touring. Still, Johannes von Trapp had enough clarity of vision to recognize that a high-energy, aerobic workout wasn't for everybody. The local aerobophiles—

the Wednesday-afternoon race crowd—might have been in it for fitness and competition. But many if not most of the lodge guests were mainly interested in simply spending time in the woods and mountains in winter.

In 1971, he had a rustic cabin built about five kilometers from the lodge in the heart of the trail network—a place for a rest, warm food and warm drink in the middle of a cross-country outing. Along with the Austrian Tea Room, closer to the lodge, the cabin was a way station providing warmth and rest for anyone interested in touring for hours at a time.

If size alone is the measure of all things, then Stowe now ranks at the top of all cross-country skiing destinations in America. Taken as a whole, the area's four cross-country centers—the Trapp

Family Lodge, Stowe Mountain Resort Cross Country Center, Topnotch Touring Center and Edson Hill Ski Touring Center—represent roughly 170 kilometers of groomed and interconnected trails, more than 100 miles. When ungroomed backcountry trails are tossed in, the trail mileage almost doubles.

By most calculations, this all adds up to the largest cross-country trail system in the United States, even if the exact definition of a groomed trail is sometimes a matter of debate. And how long this combined trail network will remain intact is also a matter of debate. At least one of the four areas, Edson Hill, with its 50 kilometers of trails, may be an endangered species, a potential victim of high-end sprawl.

The nearby Robinson Springs housing development is fast encroaching upon the Edson Hill trail system, one of the reasons

the development has been the focus of harsh local criticism. To many in the Stowe area, Robinson Springs has become the poster child for an unwelcome trend of recent years toward the construction of trophy homes for second-home owners. These homes (and the property they stand on) are not only eyesores on the landscape, according to critics, but also take away large chunks of land that were once open to such uses as hunting and skiing. Edson Hill skiing might well fall victim to the second-home trend.

But even leaving Edson Hill out of the equation, the Stowe cross-country trail network is enormous by any standard. It is also one of the most well-rounded trail networks in the country, for in addition to the many kilometers of groomed trails for aerobophiles, the backcountry opportunities are extraordinary.

Both the Trapp and the Stowe Mountain Resort trail sys-

tems connect with some of the original downhill trails cut in the 1930s. For those backcountry skiers—mostly telemarkers—who want to don climbing skins and hike up for their downhill thrills, few areas in the East can match what is available at Stowe.

Thanks in large part to the efforts of John Higgins, the long-time director of the Stowe Mountain Resort Cross Country Center, trails down Steeple Mountain and Dewey Mountain—as well as the Bruce Trail—have been cleared of overgrowth. They are essentially as skiable as they were when they were first cut. Full-day backcountry tours, to or from Bolton Valley or Underhill, are also in the mix. Johannes von Trapp's original vision of a touring center, in the true sense of the word, remains alive.

The whole Stowe trail network is not without its imperfections.

One of the biggest drawbacks is the shortage of gently rolling terrain best suited for good skate skiing. Both the Trapp and Stowe trail systems are laid out on a hillside on which trails typically rise or fall steeply. The cabin, for example, sits at an elevation of 2,100 feet, roughly 750 vertical feet above the Trapp Family Lodge. That's a fair bit of climbing (or descending) in just a five-kilometer-long trek for skiers keen on doing, say, a 20-kilometer jaunt at a consistent, aerobic pace.

Still, the popularity of Stowe as a cross-country destination is undeniable. On a typical midwinter Saturday, according to Yerrick, as many as 1,000 skiers will descend upon the Trapp Family Lodge center for at least an hour or two of skiing. On one particularly busy day in the winter of 2002, when various free promotions were being offered, the center conducted 274 free lessons.

Finally, there is the culture of cross-country skiing that has implanted itself firmly in the life of the Stowe community. It is evidenced by the popularity of such events as the Stowe Derby and the Wednesday-afternoon races, which draw a crowd even when conditions are less than ideal. "There is definitely a corps of enthusiastic cross-country skiers in this area, and it's growing," says Yerrick. He attributes at least part of that growth to an increasing number of crossover skiers—long-time downhill skiers who have decided to add cross-country skiing to their winter repertoire. The legacy of Johannes von Trapp—and of Lars Svedin and the original Scandinavian skiers of Stowe—marches on. ❖

A scene of pastoral beauty: Stowe in the early morning of a fall day.

CHAPTER 8

A Town in Transition, a Town Unchanged

For so small a town, Stowe is one mightily complex and sometimes contradictory place. It is both typical and atypical of a Vermont town, as changeless as it is ever changing. Ask any two Stowe residents to characterize their town, and they will more than likely scratch their brows with weighty forethought before giving two entirely different responses.

You might hear of Stowe described as a quaint, quiescent, quintessentially New England town, or that it is a whirring hive of tourism, sustained by the comings and goings of hundreds of thousands of visitors every year, both in winter and summer. You might hear that it is a town umbilically rooted in its past, with businesses on Main Street still run by the same families for four generations or more. Or you might hear stories, not always with a positive spin, of a vacation exurbia where Vermont rusticity has become overrun by a floodtide of second-home wealth.

You might hear, as Biddle Duke, publisher of the *Stowe Reporter* says, that Stowe is "a lot of communities within the community," all loosely but symbiotically bound together: skiers, merchants, innkeepers, farmers, contractors, tourists, artists, lawyers, well-to-do second-home owners—all manner of folk from all walks of life and all economic strata. "The social cross-pollination is so intense," says Duke of a place where extravagant wealth, thanks to those second-home owners, runs together with hand-to-mouth survival, owing to the many ski bums for whom a bed, a beer, a decent meal and a season pass represent the only necessities in a day-in-the-life.

You might hear of Stowe characterized through the prism of history: a sheep-farming town (early 1800s) that became a logging town (mid 1800s), that became a dairy-farming town (early 1900s), after which its agricultural underpinnings became gracefully but inexorably swept into the new reality of tourism.

You might hear Stowe called a ski town. It is billed as the Ski Capital of the East, after all, where in an average winter the resort registers more than 300,000 skier days, a figure representing the total number of paying customers during the course of the season. "The relationship between the mountain [i.e., the ski resort] and the community is so strong that it's hard to explain where it begins and ends," says Duke. "It's everywhere."

But then local inn and restaurant owners will tell you that summer business is now healthier than winter business; according to the 2001 Town of Stowe Annual Report, an estimated 654,000 visitors, in summer and winter, came to Stowe that year.

So to call Stowe a ski town misrepresents the four-season appeal of the place.

You might hear Stowe described as a slice of pastoral small-town Vermont. Here's the way life works in dozens of small Vermont towns and works in no small degree in Stowe as well: You do whatever is needed to get by, whether it's farming or running an inn or teaching skiing or painting houses or writing books or selling T-shirts. The idea is to cobble together some sort of income-producing existence essentially to gain the keys to the kingdom—to earn the privilege of being able to live in such an exquisitely beautiful place.

For if there is agreement on anything about Stowe, that's it: It's a beautiful place. Its principal components are drawn from the cupboard of picturesque Vermont—the town's multihued clapboard facades, its hand-painted wood signs, its oft-photographed church steeple, and the meadows and rolling hills, all framed by the massive presence of Mt. Mansfield. There is still no pollution, just as there wasn't when William Henry Harrison Bingham—a local lawyer and entrepreneur who built the Summit House—touted the clean mountain air as a tourist attraction in the mid 1800s. There are no high-rise buildings to obscure views, no neon signs to suggest tourist-trap decadence. By all outward appearances, Stowe is a reasonable facsimile of classic New England perfection.

Ed Rhodes, curator for the Stowe Historical Society, is of pure Stowe stock, the sixth generation of a family "all born a mile from the same house." He has watched the Stowe area grow signifi-

cantly, both in population and development, in the more than half century he has lived in town. "When I was growing up," he says, "there were 12 families in the Nebraska Valley (southwest of Stowe village), and I was related to 11 of the 12. Now there are over 90 families." And yet the village of Stowe itself has remained a paragon of New England changelessness. "You could bring back somebody from 1900, and they'd recognize every building," says Rhodes. "The only thing that changes in the buildings is the color of the paint."

Of course, the image of historical immutability is just that—an image. Stowe and its surroundings have changed, dramatically, significantly and with regularity, since the town was first settled in the late 18th century. When Oliver Luce, Stowe's first settler, arrived from Hartland, Vermont, on April 16, 1794, he must have had a few

moments of doubt. What he faced, as a prospective farmer, was an uninterrupted forest, from which he would need to clear a patch of arable, tillable land in order to scrape out a meager living.

Luce was exactly the sort of Bunyanesque figure one might want a first settler to be—tall and sturdy, with a deeply resonant and authoritative voice. His arrival was right out of bucolic myth—a man bearing his meager worldly possessions on an ox-drawn sled, accompanied by his wife and two children.

He cleared his land, all right, and built a one-room cabin and farmed his farm. But it was apparently rough going and not enough to advance his family's well-being to the degree he first envisioned. He lasted just 15 years before selling his farm for $2,200 and moving south to Sharon, Vermont. But by then, many other settlers had followed Luce's lead in coming to Stowe, including his brothers

Andrew, Zimri and Moses. Stowe, as a town, was on its way, riding a population explosion driven by Vermont's admission to the union. Vermont, which had gained statehood in 1791, saw its population increase 80 percent between 1790 and 1800 and another 65 percent in the following two decades.

Those early settlers in Stowe worked the land and worked it hard. Sheep farming and the production of potash sustained Stowe in its early years, as the forests gradually gave way to open land. By 1839, it was estimated that around 6,000 sheep grazed on pastureland around Stowe.

As the 1800s wore on, however, the real money to be made in Stowe was in logging and milled wood products. Among the locally made products in Stowe in the 1800s and early 1900s were butter tubs, boxes, violins and other wood instruments.

In his unpublished autobiography, *We Lived in Stowe*, Craig O. Burt, the lumber magnate, describes the logging community of Stowe near the turn of the century. Lumbering, wrote Burt, "was done…by two classes of men. The first class consists of those men willing to forgo wife or sweetheart and bury themselves for the winter in inaccessible camps back in the mountains or in the big woods… The other types who were just as necessary were the sawyers, filers, engineers and yardmen who cut the logs into lumber. The millmen were family and sweetheart men."

For the millmen and backwoods roughnecks alike, it was a life that demanded a heavy dose of self-reliance. There was no electricity, no telephone, no radio, no indoor plumbing and no mail delivery beyond the post office. In winter, snow removal was rudimentary, and a family might be stranded for several days in its

home after a heavy snowfall. You had to be ready to weather a long storm and its aftereffects, or the entire winter for that matter, as Burt explained: "Our cellar or cellarway contained a barrel of Montpelier crackers, a barrel of salt pork, salt salmon, a keg of tripe and one of corn beef, and a barrel of homemade soup. There were potatoes, beans for baking, vegetables in the vegetable bin."

As much as any story that can be told in words, the history of Stowe through the 1800s and first half of the 20th century could as easily be a story told through postcard-like images, capturing moments in time that encapsulate the character and feel of an era. Picture, for example, two men bulkily attired in buffalo-fur coats driving a team of horses through the snow. Harnessed to the horses is a giant roller 10 feet in circumference and six feet wide.

Before plowing and before the automobile—when horses and carriages were the main means of getting around—a horse-drawn roller was the customary device used to create passageways through the snow. Rather than plow the snow away, the roller would pack the snow down into a firm surface. With that, all manner of pre-automotive traffic was able to pass—oxen pulling logs to the lumberyards, horses pulling sleds, people on foot.

Visualize the burning of the Mt. Mansfield Hotel in 1889 (see page 191), an event that affirmed the cohesiveness of the community, as men, women and children came together to save the town. The citizenry gathered to form a bucket brigade, with a file of men passing full buckets, from one hand to the next, to bring water from the river to the fire, and women and children passing the empties back down to be filled. On buildings near the fire,

The Big Hotel Fire

October 4, 1889, was a fine fall day, fair and windless. It should have been a day of celebration, with fall foliage at its chromatic peak. Instead, the town of Stowe was in a panicked frenzy. The Mt. Mansfield Hotel—right on Main Street and the biggest building in town—was on fire.

While the Summit House, built atop Mt. Mansfield in 1858, was Stowe's first legitimate tourist hotel, the Mt. Mansfield Hotel (a.k.a., the Big Hotel or Big House) was the most impressive. Built in 1863 at a reported cost of $85,912.94, the Big Hotel had all the trappings of grandeur: 200 rooms, a grand ballroom, a croquet lawn, an elegant parlor, a bowling alley, and a pond with rowboats. It quickly became so popular among summer visitors from the Eastern Seaboard that another 100 rooms were added. It was also built almost entirely of wood, the construction material of choice in a town with a robust logging industry.

The cause of the fire was unknown. But once the fire had started, one thing was certain: There would be no stopping it. At best, the townspeople might contain it, preventing nearby buildings from catching fire. According to legend, a farmer spotted the beginnings of the fire from afar and, like Paul Revere announcing the coming of the British, rode through town yelling "fire!" to round up villagers. If the legend is true, the farmer was remarkably successful; in short order, a long bucket brigade was formed by the town's citizens to bring water to the fire.

Any effort to save the Big Hotel was, of course, fruitless. When the fire had run its course, the only remains were the stone chimneys and foundations and a pile of ash. But the bucket brigade did a spectacular job of preventing the spread of the fire. Miraculously, no other buildings in town burned. Even the Livery, the enormous stable adjacent to the hotel and large enough to house more than 100 horses and carriages, escaped the blaze.

An interesting subplot to the main event was the dispersal of the hotel's sizable stock of liquor. According to some stories, members of the fire brigade emptied liquor bottles into bathtubs salvaged from the hotel, and, when their work was done, filled their fire buckets with something other than water before heading home. Also, according to town historian Ed Rhodes, "The wine cellar was liberated by some French Canadians. But they didn't make it far out of town" before being apprehended by the local authorities. What happened to the wine thereafter is not a matter of historical record.

The Livery stood for another 64 years before being torn down in 1953. In the automotive age, the building had long outlived its usefulness. And even if it had survived the 1889 blaze, it was (rightfully, if ironically) deemed to be a fire hazard.

The Mt. Mansfield Electric Railroad

In the 1880s, the internal-combustion engine was in its infancy, and bus and car travel was still decades away. The main means of transportation between Waterbury and Stowe was either horse or horse-drawn vehicle, on a road surfaced with hemlock planks. But in addition to being relatively slow, horse travel had its limits. Horses were physically capable of making only a limited number of round trips per day.

For Stowe's well being, a strong transportation link to Waterbury, through which trains bearing passengers and freight passed, was vital. With electricity in the 1880s beginning to emerge as a promising power source, the towns of Waterbury and Stowe, backed by some powerful Boston businessmen, figured they had a terrific way of meeting Waterbury–Stowe transportation needs. The decision was made to build an electric-powered railroad.

The idea didn't exactly capture the public imagination at first. It took more than nine years to secure the funding and public approval at the local and state levels. But in May 1897, construction crews (mainly Italian laborers brought in just for the project and living in self-built mud huts along the route) went to work on the Mt. Mansfield Electric Railroad.

Once begun, the project began to stir local enthusiasm. That fall, an opening for the newly constructed depot in Stowe attracted more than 500 people, an event described by the local newspaper as the most elaborate of its kind ever held in Stowe. The Stowe Coronet Band played, and oysters were served. But it may have been premature; it would be another four months before the train would be in full operation.

The construction was no small engineering feat. A total of 1,100 tons of narrow-gauge track had to be laid out to cover the 12 miles between the two towns. A power plant about halfway along the line—on the Stowe side of Shutesville Hill—provided the electricity. A giant wooden trestle, 800 feet long and 60 feet high, had to be built to span a dip in the land in Waterbury Center. The total cost was $200,000, a considerable sum at that time.

The electric railroad, however, proved less successful than its original developers envisioned. It was regularly in debt, and in 1907 was sold in a bankruptcy auction to A.H. Soden, one of the original investors, for $22,500. (Soden, a Boston roofing magnate, was, among other things, an owner of the original National League baseball team in Boston.) He managed to keep the train operating (at a loss) for another 25 years, but long before its final demise, the writing was on the wall.

Buses and cars were fast becoming the preferred means of local transport in the United States, condemning many short-distance railways, like the Mt. Mansfield Electric Railroad, to obsolescence. In 1931, the railroad reported losses of $3,313.07, and the State of Vermont was planning the construction of a cement road between Waterbury and Stowe.

On May 2, 1932, the Mt. Mansfield Electric Railroad ceased operation, and the state road-construction crews didn't waste any time. They went almost immediately to work on a road that in many places followed the exact route where the train tracks had once been.

men scrambled on rooftops to douse them with water, preventing the spread of the fire. The enormous hotel burned to the ground, but the rest of the town was saved.

Imagine the excitement that must have buzzed through town with the arrival of electricity and a whole new way of life in 1911. It must have been quite a sight when the switch was flipped and the lights went on Main Street, making Stowe the first town in Vermont to have electric streetlights.

Picture young kids in the 1920s out for a bit of winter fun at a time before downhill skiing became the recreation of choice. Shortly before he died in 2000, lifelong Stowe resident Giles Dewey told the *Stowe Reporter* of tobogganing in town. "There were maybe 15 kids, and we would take a Travis sled (runners in the front and the rear with a long board in between) and we'd all

ride it down into the village," Dewey recalled. "We used to get going so fast we couldn't stop by the school, but we'd ride right up in front of the church and take a left turn on Main Street. They finally had to stop us—we went so fast and the horses couldn't get out of the way too well."

Or picture the devastation of the great flood of 1927, a cataclysmic event in Vermont history. A November deluge came atop what had already been a wet fall, and rivers throughout the state exploded over their banks. In Waterbury, south of Stowe, where the devastation was especially acute, caskets were used as emergency boats. Bridges and roads in Stowe and around the state were destroyed; in all, more than 1,000 bridges in the state were washed away, and the Central Vermont Railroad was unable to run for three months after the flood. In Stowe, in just one barn, 100

horses and cows were drowned, just a fraction of the human and animal carnage. "The whole valley was a roaring torrent," wrote Burt in *We Lived in Stowe*, "destroying roads, bridges, railroads, horses, people and cattle."

Of course such selective imagery is like looking at Stowe history through the 19th and early 20th centuries as if it were a widely gapped picket fence. The gaps are filled mostly by a normal course of day-to-day life that could have transpired in almost any Vermont town of that era, in which most people made their living off the land. Vermont, after all was (as it still is) rich in natural resources: timber on the hills and mountains, relatively fertile soil in the valleys, plentiful water in rivers and streams, and, with nature given a chance to run its course, abundant wildlife.

With their livelihood wrapped up in the land, the farmers and loggers of Stowe showed little conservational compassion and exploited the natural resources aggressively. Vermont's ecological balance took a beating as a result. At the height of the logging and farming, three quarters of the land, in Stowe as elsewhere in Vermont, was cleared of timber. By the middle of the 19th century, beaver had been hunted out of existence, and deer, moose and bear had become exceedingly rare.

It would take more than a century to reverse the impact of hunting, logging and farming, although in some cases the recovery has been remarkable. By the year 2000, more than three quarters of the land in Vermont was deemed forested, and deer, moose and bear were abundant enough for the state to have established annual hunting seasons as a means of controlling the wildlife population.

Meadow concerts at the Trapp
Family Lodge are a regular part
of the summer scene.

By the middle of the 19th century, however, Stowe added a new twist to the small-town Vermont norm of land-based economic activity. It occurred to W.H.H. Bingham that the beauty of the land, not just the resources, might have some intrinsic value. Build a hotel, Bingham figured, and tourists would come for the scenery and the fresh air, bringing their leisure dollars with them and enriching the town.

Bingham's Summit Hotel wasn't Stowe's first hotel; the Green Mountain Inn, built in 1833, claimed that distinction. But the Green Mountain Inn, at least in its early years, didn't cater to the tourist trade. Bingham's Summit House atop Mt. Mansfield, built in 1858, and his Big Hotel (as the Mt. Mansfield Hotel was locally known) built five years later in town were the real catalysts for Stowe's entry into the tourism business.

For a while, Bingham was right—the tourists with their affluence did come. Visitors would arrive by horse-drawn carriages, and some would stay for the entire summer in custom-designed suites in the Big Hotel. Among the elite classes of Boston and New York, Stowe was considered quite a fashionable place, likened to elegant Saratoga in New York. But tourism was also seasonal—who of sound mind would want to come to Vermont in the cold of winter? And the economic depressions that gripped the country in the 1870s and 1890s and during World War I didn't help matters.

So after the initial boom, tourism in Stowe ebbed, and the burning of the Big Hotel in 1889 nearly killed it. Yet logging and farming churned along steadily if not spectacularly in sustaining the town's economy. But then Roland Palmedo showed up in the early 1930s, suggesting that New Yorkers might be interested in

coming to Stowe for this *nouveau* sport called downhill skiing. He was right, of course—New Yorkers were interested—and Stowe's future as a resort town (or ski town) was cemented.

The story of Alex and Ruth Nimick is a case study of a generation of skiers who rode the Stowe wave from the early days of a fledgling ski town into the present. Theirs is not an exceptional but rather a paradigmatic story to explain Stowe's rise in popularity in the second half of the 20th century as a place not only to ski but also to settle in for the long haul. It goes something like this:

Alex Nimick, a young advertising executive in New York in the early 1940s, was bitten by the downhill-skiing bug, and Stowe by then was beginning to recapture its fashionable status thanks to skiing. Among downhill ski areas in the eastern United States, Stowe in the early 1940s was the place to go. It had the chairlift, and it had regular ski trains making the overnight trip every weekend from New York. It had Lowell Thomas, the famous broadcaster, extolling Stowe's virtues in broadcasts from the Green Mountain Inn. "If you wanted to learn how to ski, you had to go to Stowe," says Nimick. "There was no question it was the best ski area."

He rode the train from New York, as almost everyone did then; with interstate highways nonexistent and long sections of Route 100 still unpaved, driving was not an appealing or realistic option. In Stowe, Alex met Ruth, his wife-to-be, in a no-frills ski lodge called the Foster House—the start of a lifelong romance between Alex and Ruth and between the Nimicks and

Stowe. They would return again and again to Stowe for ski weekends and vacations and would eventually buy a rustic farmhouse, with no indoor plumbing and an attached outhouse, on a hill above Moscow.

They rented the house to ski instructors while Alex continued to work in New York. But in the 1960s, the Nimicks, unable to resist the lure of country life, pulled up their stakes in the New York area and moved to Stowe for good. Alex became involved with the *Stowe Reporter,* a project that helped him to establish roots within the community. That's not something that comes easily in rural Vermont, where newcomers are often viewed with a tight-lipped wariness by long-time residents. But Stowe already had a history of welcoming skiers and tourists, and the transition was relatively smooth.

The Nimicks' story is just one tile in the much larger mosaic of Stowe life. There are many stories like it—about New Yorkers or Bostonians or other East Coast migrants making the gradual transition from part-time Stowe skiers to full-time Stowe residents. It is the kind of story that explains how Stowe's growth, both in character and culture, has diverged over the second half of the 20th century from that of the typical Vermont town. And with ties to the area that reach back more than 60 years, the Nimicks have a particularly broad perspective on the changes the community has undergone in that time.

"Even back then [in the 1940s], it wasn't a hick town," says Alex. "It was a cross between a small town and a reasonably sophisticated place. But it was also a much simpler town. Beyond the Main Street area, there was very little building, even up the Mountain Road."

The evolution into a full-fledged resort town came gradually

and almost imperceptibly, says Nimick. He now looks across the valley from his new house, not far from where the old farmhouse stood, and sees houses and cleared lots where only a decade or two earlier there were forested hillsides. "None of those houses were here [when we first moved here]," he says. "Stowe is becoming a much more socially prominent place. It used to have the prestige just in winter, but now tourism is a big business in summer, too. It's a year-round operation."

He says this with slight air of sadness, as if Stowe has become too fashionable. "Most of us who live here don't want the snob value of being 'the right place,'" he says, with reference in particular to the many luxurious homes that have been built in recent years on Stowe's hillsides. But he should have seen it coming. After all, Stowe is a beautiful place—everybody agrees on that—and the

same combination of physical beauty and rural sophistication that attracted the Nimicks was sure to attract others like them.

The growing influx of outsiders—tourists, second-home owners, urban transplants —has come with tectonic inevitability, as an unstoppable force reshaping the town's look, character and economy. And the influx continues. As an exemplar of the post-Nimick generation, Jake Burton Carpenter, the man who invented snowboarding, recently moved from Burlington to the Stowe area, building a home not far from where the Nimicks live. He moved, he says, because Stowe is "right in the middle of the mountains and the schools are great, and I can't think of any place I'd rather live."

In short, as Biddle Duke says, "Stowe has become one of the places of choice to live on the Eastern Seaboard." The result has

Opposite: One reason to live in Stowe, says Jake Burton Carpenter: "The schools are great." Below: A sugarhouse in full boil. Right: Old-fashioned sugaring. Today, most sugarers collect sap through hose lines connected to trees.

been an almost complete transformation from what was principally a dairy-farming community when the Nimicks first arrived in the 1940s to a resort community today. The numbers are sometimes startling. At one time, there were about 160 farms in the Stowe area; by 1987, the official number was 13, and 15 years later there were five or fewer, depending on what you consider a farm and who's doing the counting.

A 1996 analysis of development along the Mountain Road ("Stowe Mountain Road, Past, Present and Future") reflects that change. In 1941, according to the analysis, "farming, not commerce, was the prevailing use." By 1963, "farm buildings have been converted to commercial uses... Parking lots are more prominent." And by 1994, "farm land has given way to development or been reclaimed by the forest, with large parking lots dominating the view from the road."

Ed Rhodes thinks that the completion of Interstate 89, angling through Vermont from White River Junction to the northwestern corner, was the catalyst that ushered in the modern era of tourism in Stowe. Traveling to Stowe by car from New York, Boston and other Northeastern Seaboard cities became much easier. He remembers when motels began being built on the Mountain Road in the early 1960s, at about the time when the interstate was nearing completion, and his father thinking it was "just the craziest idea." Of course 40 years later it seems anything but crazy, with more than 20 inns, lodges and motels along the Mountain Road now, all doing a brisk business in both winter and summer.

"I'll admit that Stowe isn't like a real Vermont town any more,"

The Church Beneath the Steeple

It is by no means the oldest church in Vermont, nor is it architecturally the most exemplary or unique. But the Stowe Community Church is, quite possibly, the most photographed church in Vermont. Through the hundreds of photographs published in brochures, magazines and books, the church's steeple has become almost as emblematic of Stowe as Mt. Mansfield.

But what of the church beneath the steeple? Building started in 1830, making it young by New England standards. When completed in 1863, the church, from its basement to the steeple, stood 171 feet tall.

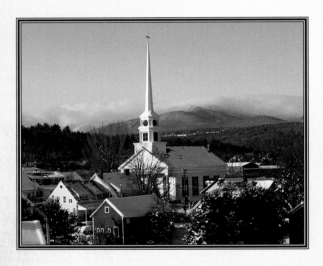

It was originally a house of worship for the Universalists, a Protestant denomination. But in 1918, the members of three other Christian religious groups—the Methodists, the Congregationalists and the West Branch Meetinghouse Society—decided to join with the Universalists in conducting services in a single house of worship. As a result, the Stowe Community Church became one of the first nondenominational churches in the country.

Rhodes says. "We lost that long ago. People don't come to Stowe to see cows and fields, and you won't really find that in Stowe." Rhodes is also not alone in worrying that the growth as a resort community and the accompanying escalation in real-estate prices have forced less affluent members of the Stowe community to look elsewhere—in Morrisville or Waterbury—to live. "I hear it all the time," he says, "'I can't afford to live in Stowe.'" Indeed, in recent years Stowe has had to institute an affordable-housing program, a measure that such posh ski resorts as Aspen and Vail have been forced to adopt to provide assistance for the many low-wage workers needed to run a town and resort.

But as some local folk bemoan the rising cost of housing and the changes wrought by tourism, the reality may be that Stowe hasn't changed as drastically as some people would like to believe. In his 1999 interview with the *Stowe Reporter*, Giles Dewey, whose grandfather came to Stowe as a farmer at the beginning of the 20th century, lent some perspective on the change. "It was probably about 1950 that I really began to feel Stowe was a tourist town," Dewey said. "It didn't develop very fast, then it started booming. I felt like the town would be ruined, but it wasn't. I still like the town."

Despite all the changes, Stowe today remains a typical Vermont town in many ways. It lies at the juncture of a pair of two-lane roads (Routes 100 and 108), as many Vermont towns do, in the midst of rolling hills and farmland. Its appearance transmits, in a way that at times seems almost premeditated to elicit soul-salving satisfaction, an aura of Grover's Corners utopia. There are the clapboard houses with their small-paned windows, the covered bridges, the muddied trucks, the deliberately low-brow manner of dress: the paint-splattered Carhartt pants, lots of flannel, work boots. Almost everybody has a dog.

Even the wealthy part-time residents play

Vermont's enduring form of governance: A town meeting of the early 1900s (left) and a town meeting (above) of more modern times.

along, for as in any Vermont town, you won't go far if you don't make some effort to fit in and adopt the unwritten local codes of conduct. Says Biddle Duke: "People are cool about being low-key and not in-your-face about wealth or about the size of their house or the power of their car. There isn't a lot of value placed in showing off."

There are no stoplights in town; small-town Vermont has an almost catholic aversion to stoplights, as if they were emblematic of some cankerous incursion of urbanization. Forget that, during the height of the ski season in winter or foliage season in fall, a stoplight at the busy intersection of Routes 100 and 108 might do wonders to relieve traffic congestion. This is rural Vermont; no stoplights allowed.

As in other Vermont towns, Stowe's governance is deter-

mined through an annual town meeting held in March. The town meeting may be a dead or dying relic in other parts of the country, but it is as vital today in Vermont as it was on March 13, 1797, the date of Stowe's first meeting. Any and all town residents are invited to participate in the process in voting on the town's budget and ordinances. And participate they do—the farmers, the merchants, the ski bums and anyone else who wants a direct say in running the town. For the town meeting of 2001, 368 residents showed up, voting on town matters large and small, from the school budget to such items as $800 for fireworks for the Fourth of July parade. It may be an antiquated and even tribal process, but it has worked for centuries in Vermont, and Vermonters, constitutionally resistant to change, see no reason to do things any differently.

Just as in any Vermont town, the day after town-meeting day in Stowe marks the unofficial beginning of the sugaring season. For the next month of so, depending on the temperatures, clouds of steam pour from sugarhouses from Morrisville to Waterbury. And after that, as the thawing effects of spring release the frozen earth from its winter bonds, the aroma of cow manure gives the air a pungent edge. Farming may be on the decline in the Stowe area, but it is still much too early to write its obituary.

"Just ask [a local farmer like] Paul Percy or Lester Pike, who still get up at five in the morning to milk the cows," says Biddle Duke. "These farms are still active and alive—as viable as their owners want to make them."

As in any Vermont town, Stowe life is defined by the transformational effects of the four seasons. Spring is about mud and maple syrup and rivers flooded with snowmelt. Summer brings an explosion of greenery and farmers' markets and a general celebration of warmth that, in boreal Vermont, is far too short-lived. Fall brings the brilliant reds, purples, yellows and oranges of the changing foliage that has justly brought worldwide fame to the state. And finally there is winter, with which Vermonters, in Stowe and elsewhere, have a love-hate relationship; they love complaining about the snow and the cold but then complain even louder when winter isn't snowy or cold enough.

In short, Stowe is just like every other Vermont town…except that it isn't. As Billy Kidd says of growing up in Stowe in the 1950s, "It was a great contrast to look at the town of Stowe next to Waterbury [to the south] or Waterville [to the north]. Those were real Vermont small towns, with no outside influence."

Left: A strong arts community is part of the complex cultural mix of the town. Below: Like all Vermont small towns, Stowe has no stoplights.

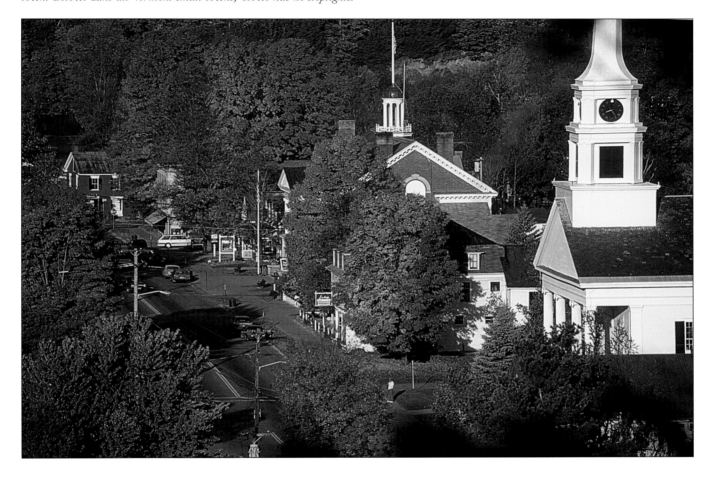

The principal "outside influence" of which Kidd speaks was ushered in by skiing, which brought a wave of first-generation Europeans. People like Sepp Ruschp and Erling Strom (see page 177) were in the vanguard, but many others followed as ski instructors, lodge proprietors and restaurateurs. They imported elements of Alpine chalet architecture, now prevalent along the Mountain Road between the village and the ski area, that are nowhere to be seen in a place like Waterbury. "I think we were just about the only native Vermonters to own a lodge in Stowe," says Kidd of his parents, who owned the Buccaneer Motel on the Mountain Road.

Tourism has bequeathed upon Stowe a cosmopolitan flourish that was a part of what attracted people like Alex and Ruth Nimick. While the village might still bear the appearance of a typical Vermont town, there's no mistaking Stowe as anything other than a tourist community along the Mountain Road, lined with restaurants, inns and shops selling everything from expensive art glass to Oriental rugs.

Of course, Stowe isn't an unmitigated microcosm of high-cultured refinement. You can still find a typically small-town place like McCarthy's, where local folk gather for breakfast to complain about the weather. But you'll also find epicurean restaurants like the Chelsea Grill or the Blue Moon Café and high-end resorts like Topnotch or the Trapp Family Lodge, all a far cry from backwater Vermont.

Still, Peter Ruschp is not alone in thinking that Stowe has done a reasonably good job of managing its growth as a resort town. "Stowe has grown, but it hasn't exploded," says Ruschp.

"Everybody in Stowe has worked together, and one of the great things we've done is that we've managed to preserve it. The chemistry and the visual appearance have remained pretty much the same. And the village still gives you that great sense of a New England community—of a classic village."

Kidd, Ruschp's childhood friend, moved to Steamboat Springs, Colorado, after retiring as a ski racer in the 1970s, and from the twin vantage points of time and distance, he hardly thinks that Stowe has been unrecognizably transformed. "When I go back, I hear people in Vermont talk about change," says Kidd. "But when compared with what's happened in places like Vail or Steamboat, the change is so small— like somebody screened in their back porch. It still looks like there are a lot of open spaces."

Indeed there are. Measuring 47,808 acres, Stowe is the largest town in Vermont in terms of area. Yet its entire population— around 4,300 in 2000—could fit comfortably on a single residential block on New York City's Upper East Side.

To many Stowe residents, that population figure represents something of a population explosion, driven in large part by the number of new homes that have been built in the area in the last decade or so. They can point to statistics for corroboration: According to the 2001 Town of Stowe Annual Report, the town comprised 1,273 primary residences and 1,234 vacation homes and condominiums, suggesting almost a 50-50 split between full-time and part-time residents.

From an historical perspective, however, this probably represents more of a redistribution of the population—from the town

center and smaller clusters to a broader distribution of homesites throughout the valley—than it does a great surge in the population. Stowe today, even with all of its part-time residents, isn't dramatically more crowded than it ever was.

The town's population over the centuries has fluctuated with its various rises and declines in economic opportunity. In 1870, with logging going strong, sheep farming still hanging on and tourism getting an early start, the town's population was 2,049. But as the sheep and logging industries ebbed gradually, so did the population in the early 1900s; it wasn't until the 1970 census, in which a population of 2,388 was reported, that the 1870 figure was surpassed.

In the more than 30 years since 1970, then, Stowe's population has increased by only slightly more than 2,000, averaging out to an annual growth rate of not much more than two percent. And despite Vermonters' notorious reputation for being stoically standoffish, the Stowe community has been reasonably accepting of the growth and change of its populus. "Stowe has always been a live-and-let-live community," says Ed Rhodes. "People aren't going to bother you. We have a lot of people from all over the world, and it's no problem. You've got to tolerate."

Other economies have come and gone in Stowe's more than 200 years of existence, and maybe the tourism economy, so robust now, will wane in the future, too. But don't count on that happening anytime soon. As long as there are mountains and snow and the colors of fall and a village that at least looks like classic New England perfection—as long as Stowe remains a beautiful place—people will keep coming, again and again. ❖

ACKNOWLEDGEMENTS

❖ ────────────────────────────────── ❖

Many people deserve credit for bringing this book into being. Bill Grout and Chris Salt, the editors at Mountain Sports Media, were expert at manipulating my raw prose into its final and publishable form. Kelley Lewis performed the immensely painstaking task of tracking down photos—in museums, libraries, and personal collections—as well as labeling them for historical accuracy. Annie Krause, as photo editor, sorted through the hundreds of possible photos in making the final selection for the book. Michelle Schrantz, as designer, blended print and photos brilliantly to give the book its striking appearance. Without the unified efforts of all of the above, this book would still be a concept rather than a reality.

I'd also like to thank Mike Colbourn, Kirt Zimmer, and Tom Hubbs at Stowe Mountain Resort for their invaluable support both in allowing me access to the resort's historical files as well as access to the mountain to experience Stowe skiing first-hand. Thanks also to Ed Rhodes at the Stowe Historical Society, Ken Biederman at the Vermont Ski Museum, Biddle Duke at the *Stowe Reporter*, Tom Sequist at the Mount Mansfield Ski Club, and the many people who agreed to be interviewed and share their Stowe experiences and memories with me.

Finally, thanks to friends, family and my father who remained patient and supportive as I rushed, often grumpily, through the winter of 2001-02 to meet deadlines. Your patience has paid off in what I think has turned out to be a handsome and readable book, in which I can take pride as the author.

❖ ────────────────────────────────── ❖

cover	Paul O. Boisvert	pp 80	Wendy Parrish Collection	pp 150	Stowe Historical Society
pp 1	Don Landwehrle	pp 81	American International Group, Inc.	pp 151	American International Group, Inc.
pp 2, 3	Don Landwehrle	pp 82 (both)	American International Group, Inc.	pp 152	Wendy Parrish Collection
pp 7	Yankee Image Collection	pp 83	American International Group, Inc.	pp 153	StoweFlake Lodge & Spa
pp 8, 9	Don Landwehrle	pp 84	Marvin Moriarty	pp 154	The Stowe Reporter
pp 11	Stu Campbell	pp 85	American International Group, Inc.	pp 155	American International Group, Inc.
pp 12, 13	Chuck Waskuch	pp 86	Special Collections, University of Vermont	pp 156	John Lord Collection
pp 14, 15, 17, 18	Don Landwehrle			pp 157	The Stowe Reporter
pp 20	Paul O. Boisvert	pp 87	Chuck Waskuch	pp 158, 159	Mt. Mansfield Ski Club
pp 21	Mike Ponte	pp 88, 89	Don Landwehrle	pp 160, 161	Yankee Image Collection
pp 22, 23	Paul O. Boisvert			pp 162, 164	John Lord Collection
pp 24, 25	Don Landwehrle	pp 90	Chuck Waskuch	pp 165	Yankee Image Collection
pp 26	Paul O. Boisvert	pp 92	Don Landwehrle	pp 166	Chuck Waskuch
pp 28 (top left)	Special Collections, University of Vermont	pp 93 (bottom left)	American International Group, Inc.	pp 167	Yankee Image Collection
		pp 93 (top left)	American International Group, Inc.	pp 168	Wendy Parrish Collection
pp 28	American International Group, Inc.	pp 93 (top right)	StoweFlake Lodge & Spa	pp 169	American International Group, Inc.
pp 29, 30	Special Collections, University of Vermont	pp 94	University of Vermont	pp 170	Green Mountain Inn
		pp 95	Julie Egenberg Collection	pp 171	Wendy Parrish Collection
pp 31 (top left)	Special Collections, University of Vermont	pp 96	Stowe Resort	pp 172 (bottom)	John Williams
		pp 97 (left to right)	Stowe Reporter; StoweFlake Lodge & Spa	(top left & right)	Stowe Reporter
pp 31	Green Mountain Inn	pp 98 (left)	Chuck Waskuch	pp 173 (bottom left)	Ski Magazine
pp 32 (top right)	Green Mountain Inn	pp 98, 99	Yankee Image Collection	(top left)	Stowe Reporter
pp 32	Green Mountain Inn	pp 100	Paul O. Boisvert	(right)	American International Group, Inc.
pp 33	Wendy Parrish Collection	pp 101	Stowe Resort	(bottom cntr.)	John Williams
pp 34, 35	Stowe Historical Society	pp 102	Paul O. Boisvert	pp 174	Don Landwehrle
pp 36 (upper right)	American International Group, Inc.	pp 103	Don Landwehrle	pp 175	Stowe Historical Society
pp 36	Wendy Parrish Collection	pp 104, 105	Yankee Image Collection	pp 176	Sandy Macy Photography
pp 37, 38	Special Collections, University of Vermont	pp 106, 107	Don Landwehrle	pp 177	New England Ski Museum
		pp 108	Stowe Reporter	pp 178	Chuck Waskuch
pp 39	Wendy Parrish Collection	pp 109, 110, 111	Yankee Image Collection	pp 179	Yankee Image Collection
pp 40	Mike Ponte	pp 112, 113	Paul O. Boisvert	pp 180	Yankee Image Collection
pp 41 (top left)	Wendy Parrish Collection	pp 114	Paul O. Boisvert	pp 181	Dennis Curran
pp 41	Wendy Parrish Collection	pp 116, 117	Mike Ponte	pp 182, 183	Don Landwehrle
pp 42	Green Mountain Inn	pp 118	Wendy Parrish Collection	pp 184	Paul O. Boisvert
pp 43	Chuck Waskuch	pp 120	Mike Ponte	pp 186	Yankee Image Collection
pp 44, 45	Don Landwehrle	pp 121	Alden Pellett	pp 187 (bottom)	Yankee Image Collection,
pp 46	John Lord Collection	pp 122	Mike Ponte	(top left)	American International Group, Inc.
pp 48	New England Ski Muesum	pp 123	Yankee Image Collection	(top right)	Yankee Image Collection
pp 49	Sherman Howe Collection	pp 124	Chuck Waskuch	pp 188	Stowe Historical Society
pp 50	Wendy Parrish Collection	pp 125	Alden Pellett	pp 189	Special Collections, University of Vermont
pp 51, 52, 53	John Lord Collection	pp 126	Chuck Waskuch		
pp 54	American International Group, Inc.	pp 127	Dennis Curran	pp 190	Green Mountain Inn
pp 55	John Lord Collection	pp 128 (both)	Rick Pavadis	pp 191	Green Mountain Inn
pp 56	Green Mountain Inn	pp 129	Chuck Waskuch	pp 193	Special Collections, University of Vermont
pp 57	John Lord Collection	pp 130, 131	Paul O. Boivert		
pp 58	Special Collections, University of Vermont	pp 131 (right)	Mike Ponte	pp 194	American International Group, Inc.
		pp 132	Paul O. Boisvert	pp 195	Don Landwehrle
pp 59, 60, 61	American International Group, Inc.	pp 133	Mike Ponte	pp 196	Green Mountain Inn
pp 62	Minot Dole	pp 134	Paul O. Boisvert	pp 197	Yankee Image Collection
pp 63	American International Group, Inc.	pp 135	Chuck Waskuch	pp 198	Don Landwehrle
pp 64	Stowe Historical Society	pp 136, 137	Don Landwehrle	pp 199 (both)	Sandy Macy Photography
pp 65	John Lord Collection	pp 138	Ski Magazine	pp 200	Yankee Image Collection
pp 66, 67	Don Landwehrle	pp 140	The Stowe Reporter	pp 201 (bottom left)	Stowe Historical Society
pp 68, 70	Julie Egenberg Collection	pp 141, 142	Julie Egenberg Collection	(top right)	Yankee Image Collection
pp 71	American International Group, Inc.	pp 143 (left to right)	Drinker Durrance; Ski Magazine	pp 202	Yankee Image Collection
pp 72	John Lord Collection	pp 144	StoweFlake Lodge & Spa	pp 203	Paul O. Boisvert
pp 74	American International Group, Inc.	pp 145	Dennis Curran	pp 204	Yankee Image Collection
pp 75	American International Group, Inc.	pp 146	John Lord Collection	pp 205	Peter Miller
pp 76	American International Group, Inc.	pp 147	New England Ski Museum	pp 214, 215	Yankee Image Collection
pp 77	Jeremy Davis	pp 148 (left to right)	American International Group, Inc.; StoweFlake Lodge & Spa	back cover	Don Landwehrle
pp 78	American International Group, Inc.				
pp 79	American International Group, Inc.	pp 149	American International Group, Inc.